Hard Press

THE MOTOR GIRLS

by Margaret Penrose

CHAPTER I

CORA AND HER CAR

"Now you've got it, what are you going to do with it?" asked Jack Kimball, with a most significant smile at his sister Cora.

"Do with it?" repeated the girl, looking at her questioner in surprise; then she added, with a fine attempt at sarcasm: "Why, I'm going to have Jim break it up for kindling wood. It will make such a lovely blaze on the library hearth. I have always loved blazing autos."

"Now, sis," objected the tall, handsome boy, as he swung his arm about the almost equally tall, and even handsomer girl, "don't get mad."

"Oh, I'm not in the least angry."

"Um! Maybe not. Put I honestly thought—well, maybe you would like some of the boys to give you a lesson or two in driving the new car. There's Wally, you know. Ahem! I thought perhaps Wally—"

"Walter can run a machine—I'm perfectly willing to grant you that, Jack. But this is my machine, and I intend to run it."

The girl stepped over to a window and looked out. There, on the driveway, stood a new automobile. Four-cylindered, sliding-gear transmission, three speeds forward and reverse, long-wheel base, new ignition system, and all sorts of other things mentioned in the catalogue. Besides, it was a beautiful maroon color, and the leather cushions matched. Cora looked at it with admiration in her eyes.

An hour, before, Jack Kimball and his chum Walter Pennington, had brought the car from the garage to the house, following Mrs. Kimball's implicit instructions that the new machine should not be driven an unnecessary block between the sales-rooms and the Kimball home.

"The car must come to Cora on the eve of her birthday," Jack's mother had stipulated to him, "and I want it to come to her brand new, with the tires nice and white. Hers must be the first ride in it."

So it was, after "digesting her surprise," as she expressed it, and spending the intervening hour in admiring the beautiful machine, climbing in and out of it, testing the levers, turning the steering wheel, and seeing Jack start the engine, that Cora was able to leave it and enter the house.

"It's—it's just perfect;" she said, with a longing look back at the car.

"Yes, and isn't it a shame mother won't let you go out in it to-night?" spoke Jack as he joined his sister at the window. "If they had only unpacked it a little earlier—it's too bad not to have a run in it while it's fresh. But," he concluded with a sigh, "I suppose I'll have to push it back in the shed."

"Yes," assented Cora, also sighing. "But mother must be humored, and if she insists that I shall not take a trial spin after dark, I'll simply have to wait until daylight. Jack, you're a dear! I know perfectly well that you influenced mother to give me this," and Cora brushed her flushed a cheek against Jack's bronzed face.

"Well, I know a little sister when I see one," replied the lad; "and though she may want to drive a motor-car, she's all right, for all that," and Jack rather awkwardly slipped his arm around his sister's waist again, for she did seem a "little sister" to him, even if she was considered quite a young lady by others.

"Girls coming up to-night?" asked Jack after a pause, during which they both had been silently admiring the car and its graceful lines.

"I don't know," replied Cora. "They haven't heard about my new auto, or they'd be sure to come."

"Let's run over and tell them," proposed Jack.

Cora thought for a moment. She had plans for the evening, but they did not include Jack.

She said finally: "I have to write a few letters—acknowledging some birthday gifts. Don't wait for me if you intend to go over to Walter's. You might call at the Robinsons', however, to fetch me; say at half-past nine."

"Oh, then I'm not to see Bess or Belle—or—well, there are plenty of other girls just as keen on ice cream sodas as those mentioned," and he pretended to leave the room, as if his feelings had been hurt.

"Now; you know, Jack, I always want you with me, but—"

"But just to-night you don't. All right, little sister. After me running that machine up from the garage for you, and not even scraping the tires; after me—even kissing you! Fie! fie! little girl. Some day you may want another machine—or a kiss—"

"Children, children," called Mrs. Kimball, "are you coming to dinner? And are you going to put that machine in the shed before dark, Jack?"

"Both—both, mum! We were just discussing a discussion about the—the machine, girls and ice cream sodas."

"What nonsense!" exclaimed his mother with a laugh. "Come to dinner, do. But, Jack, run the machine in first, please."

The car was put under a shed attached to the barn, Cora looking enviously at Jack as he manipulated the levers and wheels, she sitting on the seat beside him, on the short run up the driveway. She would not venture to operate it herself in such cramped quarters.

"There!" exclaimed Cora as Jack locked the shed door. "I hope nobody steals it to-night. Did you take out the plug, Jack?"

"Here you are," and he handed her the brass affair that formed the connection for the ignition system, and without which the car could not be run. "Put it under your pillow, sis," he added. "Maybe you'll have a gasolene dream."

They went into the house, where dinner was waiting for them. The meal was a simple one, although the means of the little family were ample for a most elaborate affair. But Mrs. Kimball preferred the elegance of simplicity.

Mrs. Grace Kimball was a wealthy widow, a member of one of the oldest and best known families in Chelton, which was a New England town, not far from the New York boundary. Her husband had been Joseph Kimball, a man of simple tastes and sterling principles. When he had to leave her, with the two children, he said as he was passing away:

"Grace, I know you will bring them up rightly—plainly and honestly."

Plain in character, upright and fair, the two children had grown, but, in personality, nothing could make either Jack or Cora Kimball "plain." They were just simply splendid.

"Then I can't take out the machine to-night, mother dear?" asked Cora after dinner.

"Not to-night, daughter. I know you can run a car, but this is a new one, and I would feel better to have you give it a test run in daylight. You must get the man at the garage to show you all about it. Do you like it very much, Cora?"

"Like it! Oh, mother, I perfectly love it! I can scarcely believe it is all mine—that Jack has no mortgage on it and that it's my very own."

"I don't know about that," put in Jack. "A fine car like that is rather a dangerous thing for a handsome young lady of seventeen summers, and some incidental winters, to go sporting about in. Some one else may get a mortgage on it, and want to foreclose."

"Now, I don't tease you, Jack," objected his, sister, "and a girl has just as much right to tease a boy as a boy has to tease a girl."

"Goodness me! You don't call that teasing, do you? The girls have all the rights now. But help yourself! I'm not particular. Did you say I was to call at the Robinsons' at nine?"

"No, nine-thirty."

"Oh, exactly. Well, I'll try to be there. You might make it a point not to be waiting on the drive for me. A fellow wants to get a look at a girl like Bess once in a while—just for practice, you know."

"Oh, Jack!"

"Oh, Cora! What's the matter?"

"You're horrid!"

"All right. Then I'm going off and read a horrible tale about pirates, and walking the plank, and all that. I'll be on hand at the time and place mentioned. Hoping this will find you well, remain, yours very truly, Jack." And he hurried out of the room amid the laughter of his mother and sister.

"What a boy!" exclaimed Mrs. Kimball.

It was a pleasant, summer evening, and when Cora hurried down the avenue toward the Robinson home, she actually seemed to have wings. For she was not running, and her pace could hardly be called walking.

Her tall, straight figure was clad in a simple linen gown. She had need to disregard frills now, for she was a motor girl.

"Oh, come on, and don't ask a single question!" she exclaimed as the Robinson twins—Bess and Belle—hastened to meet her in response to her ring. "Come on! We must go over to the garage, quick! I've got a new machine, and I've got to learn all about it."

She had to pause for breath, and Belle managed to say

"Cora! A new machine! All for yourself! Oh, you dear! Who gave it to you?"

"Why Jack found it," Cora laughed. "It was running along the street, you know, and he lassoed it. It was going like mad, but he whirled the lash of his riding-whip about it and—and—"

"Now, Cora, dear!" and Belle dropped her voice to one of aggrieved tones. "You know what I meant."

"Of course I do, girly; but hurry—do! I want the man at the garage to teach me all about my new machine. I call it the Whirlwind.' You know it's different from Jack's small runabout, and there are several new points to be posted on. I want to be all ready, so that when we go out to-morrow morning we can surprise the boys."

"Oh, how perfectly lovely!" exclaimed Bess.

Delighted and excited, the three girls hurried over the railroad hill, on a short cut to the garage.

"Do you think he'll show you?" asked Bess. "He might want you to hire a chauffeur."

"Well, we'll see," responded Cora. "If we can manage to find a nice, agreeable, elderly gentleman—the story-book kind of machinist, you know. I fancy he will be sufficiently interested— ahem! well, you know—" and she finished with a little laugh; in which her chums joined.

They had reached the small door of the office of the garage. A notice on the glass directed them to "Push."

Cora put both hands to the portal, and it swung back. She almost stumbled into the room.

"We would like to see some one who will teach us how to run an auto," she began. "I know something of one, but I have a new kind."

The three girls drew back.

"A nice, agreeable, elderly gentleman!" whispered Belle to Cora.

Cora could not repress a smile.

Instead of the "story-book machinist," a handsome young lad stood before them, smiling at their discomfiture.

"What is it?" he asked in a pleasant voice, and Cora noticed how white and even his teeth were.

"We—er—I—that is, we—I want to learn some points about my new car," she stammered. "It's a—"

"I understand," replied the handsome chap. "I will be very glad to show you. Just step this way, please," and, with a little bow, he motioned to them to follow him into the semi-dark machine shop back of the office.

CHAPTER II

THE DASH OF THE WHIRLWIND

When Jack Kimball called at the Robinson home that same evening, at precisely nine-thirty, he found three very much agitated young ladies. Bess, or, to be more exact, Elizabeth Robinson, the brown-haired, "plump" girl—she who was known as the "big" Robinson girl—was positively out of breath, while her twin sister, Isabel, usually called Belle, too slim to puff and too thin to "fluster," was fanning herself with a very dainty lace handkerchief.

Cora paced up and down the piazza, in the true athletic way of cooling off.

"Why the wherefore?" asked Jack, surprised at the excitement so plainly shown, in spite of the girls' attempts to hide it.

"Oh, just a race," replied Cora indifferently.

"Out in the dark?" 'persisted Jack.

"Only across the hill," went on Cora, while Bess giggled threateningly.

"Seems to me you took a queer time to race," remarked the lad with a sly wink at Isabel. "Who won out?"

"Oh, Cora, of course," answered Isabel. "She won—in and out."

"Oh, I don't know," spoke Jack's sister. "You didn't do half badly, Belle."

"Oh, I was laughing so I couldn't run."

"Cora said you were coming for her," put in Bess with a smile.

Jack seemed disappointed that the subject was mentioned.

"Yes," he said. "She was very particular to specify the time. It's nine-thirty now, but I'm in no hurry," and he looked about for a chair.

"But I am," insisted Cora.

"Well, then," added Jack a bit stiffly, "if you're ready, suppose we run along. Or, have you had enough running for this evening?"

"Plenty. But I really must go, girls. Be sure and be ready in the morning for—well, you know what," and she finished with a laugh. "We want the Chelton folks—"

"To sit up and take notice, I suppose," put in Jack quickly. "Pardon the slang, ladies, but sometimes slang seems to fit where nothing else will."

The twins managed to whisper a word or two into Cora's ear as she said good-night and left with her brother.

They had had such a splendid time at the garage. It was the run back home, over the railroad embankment, that had caused all their flurry and excitement. And, though they had not left the auto salesrooms until five minutes before the time Cora had appointed for her brother to meet her, they had actually managed to reach home before Jack called, so that he could have no suspicion of their visit to the garage.

Paul Hastings, the young man whom they had encountered on their visit to the automobile place, had proved a most interesting youth—he appeared to know many things besides the good and bad points of the average car.

Mr. and Mrs. Perry Robinson, parents of the Robinson twins, happened to be out that evening, so that, even to them, the visit to the garage was a profound secret, and there was no need of making any explanations.

That night, in her sleep, Elizabeth was heard to mutter "The clutch! Throw in the clutch!"

And Isabel actually answered, also in dream language:

"Jam down the brake!"

But Cora, across the fields, in her own cool, out-of-doors sleeping apartment, built on a broad porch, did not dream. She just slumbered.

It was a delightful morning in early June, and the air seemed sprinkled with scented dew, when Cora Kimball drove up to the Robinson home in her new automobile.

"Come on! Come on!" she called as she stopped at the curb and, tooted the horn. "Hurry! I want to overtake Walter. He and Jack have just gone out!"

"Oh, of course, you want to overtake Walter," answered Isabel, with the emphasis on "Walter."

"Well, never mind about that, but do come," urged Cora. "What do you think of my car?" she asked as the girls hastened to her. "Isn't it a beauty?"

She handled the machine with considerable skill, for she had had some practice on Jack's car.

"Think of it!" exclaimed Elizabeth. "Why, it's simply beyond thoughts; it's—overwhelming!"

"A perfect dream," agreed Belle. "Aren't you the lucky girl, though!"

"Guess I am," admitted Cora. "See, I can start it without cranking"; and to prove it, when the engine was quiet, she threw forward the spark lever, shifted the gasolene one a trifle, and the motor began to throb and hum rapidly.

"Good!" cried Isabel.

"Paul told me about it," went on Cora. "The Paul, you know. He said when a charge of gas is in one of the cylinders all you have to do is to send a spark to the cylinder, and—"

"It didn't take you long to learn," complimented Bess, while Isabel said:

"Paul—er—is he—"

"Yes, he is," admitted Cora with a laugh. "The youth of the garage."

"Well, I don't remember a thing he said," confessed Elizabeth; "but Paul—who could forget Paul? Didn't he have nice teeth?"

"And so polite," added Belle.

"Wasn't he just splendid?" concluded Cora. "And such a number of things that he told me. But come on, get in," and she slowed down the motor somewhat, while, removing a pair of buckskin gloves from her long, tapering hands, she produced a small, dainty handkerchief and rubbed a spot of black grease from her aristocratic nose.

"Got that when I was oiling the rear wheels," she explained.

The twins entered the tonneau, neither of them caring to risk riding on the front seat just yet.

Cora speeded the motor up a bit, glanced behind to see that the tonneau door was securely fastened, and then pulled the speed lever and threw in the clutch. The car started forward as smoothly as if Paul himself were at the wheel.

Elizabeth's hand flew to her hat, which tilted backward in the wind. They had not yet secured their motor "togs," and regulation hats were so difficult to manage.

"Oh, isn't this glorious!" cried Isabel.

"Every one is looking at us," announced Elizabeth.

"Now I wonder which road Jack and Walter took?" said Cora as she swung the car around a curve in good style. "I heard Jack say he was going for some fishing-tackle."

"Perhaps they went to Arden," ventured Isabel.

"Maybe. Well, we'll take a nice little spin down the turnpike," decided Cora as she threw in the high gear, the cogs grinding on each other rather alarmingly.

"Gracious! What's that?" asked Elizabeth.

"Only the gears," replied Cora calmly. "I hope I didn't strip them, but I might have done that changing a little better. I wasn't quite quick enough."

The car was going rather fast now.

"Don't put on quite so much speed," begged Isabel. "I'm so—"

"Now please don't say you're nervous," interrupted Cora.

"But I am."

"Well, you needn't be. I know how to run the car."

"Of course, since Paul showed her," put in Elizabeth.

The speed was a trifle too fast for an inexperienced hand at the wheel, but Cora grasped the wooden circlet firmly, and with a keen look ahead prepared for the descent of a rather steep hill.

Coming up the grade were a number of autos, containing Chelton folks, who had been to the depot with early city commuters. Chelton was a great place for commuters and autos.

"Please don't put on any more speed, Cora," again begged Isabel, leaning over toward the front seat. "This is such a steep hill."

"All right, I won't," and Cora placed her foot more firmly on the brake pedal, while she was ready to grasp the emergency lever quickly, in case anything happened.

"Oh, there's Ida!" suddenly cried Elizabeth as a small runabout loomed up in front of them.

"And Sid Wilcox. I wonder what she finds interesting in that—that lazy chap?"

"A companion—that's all," replied her sister. "I think Ida is about as unenergetic a girl as I ever knew."

"Funny thing," said Cora, speaking loudly enough to be heard above the noise of the motor, "how she manages to keep going. She rides as often in Sid's car as if—well, as if she was his own sister."

"Oftener than most sisters," added Belle significantly.

"They have just left her friend, who was on from New City, at the depot," said Bess. "It's quite handy to have a chum with a motor-car—even if it does happen to be a chap like Sid."

"Well, I guess Ida's harmless, even if she is jealous," said Cora. "I do believe that's all that ails Ida—just plain jealousy."

"Maybe," assented Isabel.

They rode along for some time, coasting down the steeper parts of the hill, and running easily where there was a level stretch. They were now approaching the worst part of the descent. From this point there was quite a steep slant to the level highway, which the railroad crossed at grade, and approached on a curve.

There was a long-drawn, shrill whistle.

"What's that?" exclaimed Elizabeth.

"The train!" cried Isabel. "Oh, the train! Cora, the train is coming!"

"I hear it," spoke Cora calmly, but she pressed her foot down harder on the brake pedal, and tried to use the compression of the cylinders as a retarding force, as Paul had showed her.

"Can't you slow up?" pleaded Elizabeth. There was a note of alarm in her voice.

"I'm—I'm trying to!" almost shouted Cora, as she exerted more strength on the brake lever. "I've done all I know, now, but but we don't seem to be stopping!"

She spoke the last words in a curiously quiet voice.

"Put on the brakes!" called Bess.

"They are on!" said Cora fiercely.

"Oh, Cora!" screamed Isabel. "I see the train! There at the foot of the hill! We'll run into it! I'm going to jump! We can't stop!"

"Sit still!" commanded Cora energetically.

Elizabeth covered her face with her hands. She shrank back into her seat. Her sister leaned up against her. Below could be heard the puffing of the train. Then the engineer, seeing the auto rushing down to destruction, blew shrieking whistles, as if that could help.

Cora was frantically pulling on the brake lever. Her face was now white with fear, but even in the midst of this terror she felt a curious calmness. It was just as if she were looking at some picture of the scene. She thought she was miles and miles away. Her foot was pressed down so hard on the brake pedal that it felt as if her shoe would burst off.

But the car slid along, nearer and nearer the track, along which the train was thundering—rushing to meet the auto-to annihilate it.

"Stop! Stop!" screamed Isabel. "Stop!" She rose in her seat.

"Sit down!" commanded Cora.

"But stop!" pleaded Isabel. "We'll all be killed! Stop! Oh, Cora, stop!"

"I'm trying to!" was the grim reply. "But—I can't the brake—the brake is jammed!"

The last words came out jerkily, for Cora was pulling on the brake handle with all her force.

Nearer and nearer sounded the approaching train. The auto was sliding down the hill with ever-increasing speed, but Cora never let go her hold of the steering wheel.

Once more she tried to pull the brake lever. It would not come back another notch. The engineer of the train was blowing more frantic signals. He leaned from his cab window and motioned the auto back. He even seemed to be shouting to them.

Cora braced both feet against the brake pedal.

She took a firmer grasp of the wheel. The seams of her new gloves were starting from the strain. There was a desperate look on her face.

"Oh, we'll be killed! We'll be killed!" screamed Isabel. "We can't get across in time!"

She leaned over, and fell into her sister's arms, while Cora, with a keen glance to either side, stiffened in her seat. There was a bare chance of safety.

CHAPTER III

A SUDDEN ACQUAINTANCE

Despite the tense moment of anxiety, the almost certainty that the auto would crash into the train, Cora's quick eye had seen something that she hoped would enable her to avert the accident.

She knew that she could not stop the machine in time, by any means at her command. There was but one other thing to do. That was to steer to one side.

To the left there was a solid stone wall. To dash into that would mean almost as horrible an accident as if she collided with the train. To the right there was a field, but it was fenced in, and between it and the road was a little miry, brook.

In some places the brook widened almost into a pond. The bottom was treacherous, and to steer into it meant to sink down deeply into the mud. To run into the fence might mean that one of the rails would become entangled in the mechanism of the motor, tearing it all to pieces. Or one of the long pieces of wood might even impale the occupants of the car.

Cora's eyes swept down the length of the barrier with a flash.

There was just what she wanted! A gap in the fence!

She could go through that in safety. But suppose the machine was brought to too sudden a stop in the mud? They would all be thrown out and perhaps injured. But it was the only thing to do.

With a firm grasp of the wheel Cora sent the auto from the road.

Elizabeth screamed as she felt the swaying of the car. She had to hold her sister from being tossed but, for Isabel was incapable of taking care of herself.

Straight for the field rushed the car, the engineer of the train now tooting his whistle as if in gladness at the narrow escape.

Splash!

The auto fairly dived into the brook, and gradually slackened speed. Right toward a clump of willow trees it surged, throwing a spray of water in advance. Then it became stationary in the middle of a spot where the brook widened into a pond.

Cora was dimly conscious of a figure on the opposite bank of the stream. A figure of a young man, with a fishing-pole in his hands. She saw a spray of water, cast up by the auto, drench him. She even heard him cry out, but at that moment she gave him not a thought.

Everything centered on her narrow escape, the condition of her two chums, and, last, but not least, whether her new auto had been damaged.

Cora leaned over the side and looked at the water flowing past the mud guards.

"Safe!" she exclaimed. "I—I thought we were doomed, girls. Didn't you?"

"Doomed?" echoed Elizabeth. "I never want to go through that experience again."

"Me either," added Cora fervently. "Has Belle fainted?"

"I'm afraid so."

Cora leaned over, scooped some water up in her hand, and dashed it into the white face of the girl. Isabel opened her eyes.

"Are we—are we—" she gasped.

"We're all right, you little goose," said Cora with a laugh, though her voice trembled and her hands shook. "I guess it wasn't nearly as dangerous as it looked."

"It was bad enough," spoke Elizabeth.

"Anyhow, the auto stopped," went on Cora. "Don't you see where we are? In the middle of Campbell's Pond. And we won't have to swim out, either. It's not very deep. But, Bess, you look like a sheet, and Belle, you seem like—"

"A pillow-case, with the pillow out," added Isabel with a wan smile. "I never was so glad to get a ducking in all my life."

"And I guess we're not the only ones who got a ducking," said Cora as she shook some drops from her hair.

"Why?" inquired Bess.

"Look!" and Cora pointed across the pond. A very much drenched figure was standing up. The man with the fishing-pole was wiping the water from his face. He looked at the girls in the auto.

"Oh, dear!" exclaimed Elizabeth. "I should think we did give him a ducking!"

"I'm awfully sorry, but—but we couldn't help it," said Cora, standing up and looking at the young man.

He approached closer, began wading out into the pond toward the auto. The water was not very deep, hardly up to his knees. Cora found herself wondering how he had managed to fish in it.

He was very good-looking, each of the girls was thinking to herself.

"Can't I help you?" he asked, smiling broadly, in spite of the mud and water splashed all over him. There was actually a little globule of mud on the end of his nose. He seemed as much amused over his own predicament as he was over that of the motor girls. "Do you need any help?" he went on.

"I'm sure I—er—that is, I hardly know," stammered Cora. She was not altogether certain about the state of the auto. "I'm afraid we've been very—very impolite—to splash water, and—er—mud all over you," she added.

"Not at all—not at all," he assured her. "I never saw a better—a better turn, so to speak. You are very plucky, if I may be permitted to say so. I—er—I almost said my prayers when I saw you racing down toward the train. Then I saw you turn in here. But what happened that you couldn't stop before?"

"The brake," replied Cora. "It refused to work. This is a new car—our first trip, in fact."

"Oh, I see," replied the young man. "Well, I know a little about cars. Perhaps I can run her out for you. Just let me try."

Cora shifted over to the other side, leaving the wheel free. The young fisherman cranked up, from a very insecure and muddy footing in the middle of the pond. There came a welcome "Chug! chug! chug!"

The auto was all right, after all.

The young man climbed in. The spot of mud was still on his nose, and Cora felt an insane desire to laugh. But she nobly restrained it. He took the wheel and threw in the low speed gear. There was a grinding sound, the Whirlwind seemed to shiver and shake, and then it began to move. A few seconds later, after running slowly through the pond, it ran up the soft bank, and, under the skilful touch of the stranger, came to a stop in a grassy meadow.

"There!" exclaimed the young man. "I guess you're all right now. But let me look at that brake. Perhaps I can fix it."

Then it occurred to Cora that she might attempt to introduce her friends and herself. The twins had not yet spoken a word to the fisherman.

The same thought "wave" must have surged into the stranger's brain, for he said:

"My name is Foster—Edward Foster," and he raised his wet cap. "I was just trying to kill time by fishing, but it was a cruelty to time. I don't believe a fish ever saw this pond."

"Mr. Foster, my name is—er—Kimball—Cora, Kimball," said the owner of the auto, imitating the young man's masculine style of introduction, "and these are my friends, the Misses Robinson."

The young man bowed twice, once for each of the twins. Mr. Foster had a most attractive manner—that was instantly decided by the three girls.

"I know your brother," he remarked to Cora. "Jack Kimball, of Exmouth College."

"Oh, yes, of course. I've heard Jack speak of you, I'm sure."

"Yes, he was on our team—"

"Oh, you are the great football player," interrupted Elizabeth. She made no secret of her admiration for "great football players."

"Not exactly great," answered Mr. Foster, "but I have played some. My interest in sports has rather kept me away from society. That accounts for me not being better acquainted in Chelton, or perhaps—"

"Hello there!" came a hail from the road.

"Jack and Walter!" exclaimed Cora, as at that moment another machine came along and drew up alongside the fence which separated the highway from the meadow. "Now, won't they laugh at us!"

"Well, I declare!" exclaimed the mud-bespattered young fellow. "If that isn't Jack! And Walter Pennington is with him!"

"What's up?" called Jack, leaping from the car and running across the meadow, after a quick climb over the fence.

"A great deal is up," said Cora.

"Well—Ed Foster! Where in the world did you come from?" Jack added as he saw the young man about to alight from Cora's car.

"From the ditch," was Ed's laughing answer, as he looked down at his splattered garments. "I just got but in time to—"

"Never mind—shake!" interrupted Jack, extending his hand. "When I was a youngster, and our big Newfoundland dog came out With the stick from the pond—"

"Now! now!" cautioned Ed. "I may be big, and I may have just crawled from the pond, but I deny the stick."

"I'm sure we would have been here forever if Mr. Foster hadn't—" began Cora.

"Been here first," interrupted Jack. "That's all very well, sis. But I told you so! A brand-new, spick-and-span car like this! And to run it into a muddy ditch!"

"Indeed!" exclaimed Elizabeth. "We were almost killed! Cora just saved our lives!"

"Mercy me!" cried Walter, who had left the car and joined Jack. "Now, Cora," he added mockingly, "when you start out to save lives, why don't you give a fellow the tip? There's nothing I do so love as to see lives saved—especially nice young ladies," and he made a low bow.

"Oh, you may laugh," said Cora somewhat indignantly, "but I don't want anything like it to happen again. The brake would not work, and—"

"The train was just in front of us, and we were running right in it," put in Isabel, her voice far from steady, and her face still very white.

At this point Ed insisted upon telling the whole story, and he described the plight of the motor girls so graphically that both Jack and Walter were compelled to admit that Cora did indeed know how to drive a car in an emergency, and that she had acted most wisely.

"Good for you, sis!" exclaimed Jack, when the story Was finished. "I could not have done better myself."

"Such praise is praise indeed," spoke Ed with a laugh.

He went around back to look at the brake, and found what had caused the trouble. A loose nut had fallen between the brake band and the wheel hub, and prevented the band from tightening. The trouble was soon remedied, and the brake put in working order.

"There—you are all ready for the road now," remarked Ed.

"Thank you—very much," said Cora quietly, but there was a world of meaning in her tones.

Ed looked into her eyes rather longer than perhaps was necessary.

"Come on; get in with us, Ed," invited Jack. "Haven't seen you in an age. Let's hear about the Detroit team."

"Oh, I'm—I'm too dirty to get in the car, I'm afraid," objected Ed, with a glance at the mud spots that were now turning to light-gray polka-dots on his clothes, in the strong sunlight.

"Nonsense!" cried Jack heartily. "Come along. Walter will drive for Cora, in case she is nervous. It needs a strong wrist in this soft ground."

"Oh, yes! Do please steer for us," begged the still trembling Isabel. "I'd feel so much safer—"

"Well, I like that!" cried Corm with a light laugh. "Is that the way you treat me, after having saved your life?"

"But it was you-who—who almost ran us into the train, Cora," answered Isabel, giving her friend a little pinch on her now rosy cheek. "So you see it was your duty to save us."

"Well, I did it," replied Cora, glad that she had come out of the affair with such flying colors.

Walter took Ed's place at the steering wheel of the Whirlwind, and the fisherman seated himself beside Jack. Then Walter ran Cora's car out of the mire of the meadow and into the road, the three girls remaining in the machine.

"I suppose if the young ladies hadn't run you down we wouldn't have seen you the entire summer," said Jack to Ed as he ran the smaller machine along behind the touring car.

"Oh, indeed you would," answered Ed. "I really intended looking you up in a day or two. You see, I have been very busy. What are you laughing at? Because I said I was busy? Well, I guess I have the busiest kind of business on hand. Say, let me whisper," and he leaned over confidentially, though there was no need for it, as the other auto was some distance ahead. "I'm going into finance."

"Finance?"

"Yes. Stocks—bonds—and so on, you know. Bank stocks. Think of that, Jack, my boy!"

"Good for you! Three cheers for the bank stock!" exclaimed Jack in a half whisper. "In the new bank, I suppose?"

"The correct supposition," answered Ed. "I have been invited to subscribe for some of the new issue of stock, and I've decided to. I'm going over to get it in a day or two. I'm to pay partly in cash, and turn over to them some of my bonds and other negotiable securities that I inherited from father, who was a banker, you know. I think I am making a good investment."

"Not a bit of doubt about it," said Jack. "I wish I had the chance."

"I hear that Sid Wilcox wanted to get some of the stock, Jack," went on Ed. "He comes of age soon, and he will have some cash to invest. But, somehow, there's a prejudice against Sid. He has not been asked to take stock, though the directors rectors know he has money."

"Well, I guess the trouble is he can't be depended on. He'd be peddling the stock all over the State, or putting it up for doubtful transactions, and I guess the directors wouldn't like that. He's a reckless sort. I shouldn't mind his fits of crankiness, if he would only leave girls out. But when he goes in for some kind of mischief harmless in itself, he invariably brings some girl into it, and she has to suffer in the scrape with him. It's not right of Sid. But—speaking of angels—there he is now."

Jack's runabout, called the Get There, had been climbing the hill back of the Whirlwind, and both machines were now on a level stretch of road and approaching Fisher's store—an "emporium," as the sign called it, and a place where one could get anything from a watch to a shoestring, if old Jared Fisher only knew that it was wanted before he went to town.

It so happened, however, by some strange intervention of providence, that he never did know in time. But, at any rate, you could always get soda water—the kind that comes in the "push-in-the-cork bottles," and that was something.

As the two autos drew up, the occupants beheld, standing on the steps of the store, Sidney Wilcox and Ida Giles. Jack halted his car behind the Whirlwind.

"Hello there!" called out Ed. "Seems to me I'm bound to meet all my friends today. How are you, Sid?"

Ed leaped from Jack's car and up the steps to greet Sid.

"Oh, I'm so-so," was the rather drawling answer. "But what's the matter with you? Been clamming?"

23

"Not exactly," replied Ed, glancing down at the mud spots; "but I caught something, just the same."

"So I see," responded Sid, chuckling at his wit. "Pity to take it all, though. You should have left some for the turtles. They like mud."

Jack, who followed Ed, said something in conventional greeting to Ida. But the girl with Sid never turned her head to look in the direction of the Whirlwind. Cora remarked on this in a low voice to Isabel and Elizabeth.

"I hear that you are going in for—er—Wall Street," said Sid to Ed in rather a sarcastic voice.

"Oh, no. Nothing like that. No chance for a lamb like me in Wall Street. It's too much of a losing game."

"Oh, I don't know," drawled Sid. "A fellow might make good, and then do—well, better."

Ed glanced at Jack. How did Sid know about Ed's plan to take stock in the new bank? That was a question that each youth flashed to the other.

There was something unpleasant in the manner of Sidney Wilcox. All in the party seemed to feel it. And as far as the girls were concerned, they noticed much of the same manner in Ida, though Jack and Ed were not quite so critical. As for Walter, he did not seem to be giving Ida a thought. But it is doubtful if she was so indifferent toward him. Still, she would not look in his direction while Cora and her two chums were with him.

Corn walked slowly up the broad store steps; Bess and Belle following.

"I'm simply choked," said Cora with a laugh. "I never had such a thirsty run."

Ida seemed very much interested in the distant landscape.

"The roads are awfully dry," she murmured.

"And so am I," added Elizabeth as she followed her sister and Cora into the store. Walter and Jack trailed in after them, while Ed stayed for a moment outside with Ida and Sid. The latter did not introduce Ed to Ida. It was a habit Sid had, of never presenting his young men chums to his "girl," unless he could not avoid it. Ida, perhaps, knew this, and she strolled to the other end of the porch.

"How'd you make out in your exams?" asked Ed of Sid, for the latter attended college with Jack. That is, he was in his study class, though not in the same grade socially.

"Oh, pretty fair. I cut most of 'em. I finish next year, and I don't intend to get gray hairs over any exams now."

"You cut 'em?" repeated Ed.

"Sure," and Sid started toward his car, Ida following. "So long."

"Well, you're not going away mad, are you?" asked Ed with a laugh, wondering the while over the identity of the striking-looking girl whom Sid so obviously refrained from introducing to him.

"Oh, not's so's you could notice it," was Sid's answer as he began to tuck the dust robe over Ida's lap.

Then Sid cranked up his car, which he had named the Streak, though it didn't always live up to the name, and soon he and the girl were out of sight around a turn in the road.

"Humph!" exclaimed Ed as he entered the store. "I wonder where he heard about my plan to take—bank stock? I wish he didn't know of it. And I also wonder who that pretty girl was?" For Ida was pretty, in spite of her reddish hair and her rather jealous disposition, which was reflected in her face.

Ed shook his head. He was puzzled over something.

CHAPTER IV

TWENTY THOUSAND DOLLARS

"Say, Jack," remarked Ed a few days later, when the two were sprawled beside a brook, with rod and reel, "I believe I'll have to get better acquainted with the young folks out here. Honestly, I feel wobbly when I get to talking to them. I've been out of touch with them so long that I'm afraid I'll ask after some dead and gone aunt or uncle, or for some brother that has been in trouble and isn't spoken of any more in polite society. For instance, who is Ida—Ida Giles? You know—the girl who was with Sid? He introduced me to her last night."

"Oh, Ida—why—she's—just Ida. That's all. But that's a good idea of yours. I was thinking myself that you ought to begin studying up the blue-book of Chelton society. Now, as to Ida, the red-haired girl—"

"Not really red," corrected Ed slowly, "but that bright, carroty shade—so deliciously like lobster a la—"

"Oh, pardon me," and Jack assumed an affected manner. "Of course, Ida's hair is not really red—not merely—carroty is the very word needed. Well, she is the daughter of the Reverend Mrs. Giles. Don't you remember the woman who always scolded us for everything? Wouldn't let us even so much as take a turnip. And she wore such pious-looking spectacles that we dubbed her Reverend Mrs. Giles. Well, she still is Ida's mother."

"Then I don't blame Ida a bit. I'd be Ida myself if I was brought up as she's been, though I suppose her mother means all right. It's curious what queer manners some people have. But I dare say we all have our own faults."

"And, with all of them, I hope the girls love us still—even Ida," added Jack quickly.

"Now, those others—the beautiful Robinson twins," pursued Ed.

"Oh, yes. Well, Bess and Belle are certainly the real thing in girls—right up to the minute. Besides, they have an immensely rich papa. You've heard of him—Perry Robinson, the railroad king?"

"Oh, yes. And their mother, if one may be permitted to ask?"

"Certainly, fair sir—Their mother is a wonderfully handsome woman, in a statuesque sort of way. Very dignified, and all that. Now, the twins are worth while."

"Exactly so," answered Ed. "Now I think—"

He stopped suddenly, and quickly jerked up his rod, but not quite speedily enough, for he had the pleasure of seeing a fish slip wrigglingly off the hook.

"Biggest one to-day," he murmured as he adjusted some fresh bait. "Now, as to the Robinson twins. The only fault I have to find with them, from my limited acquaintance, is that they are not evenly divided. Bess is—er—well, not to be too delicate about it—too fat—"

"No, no, I beg of you!" exclaimed Jack. "Don't use that word. Say too much adiposed."

"Sounds like indisposed," murmured Ed; "but let it go at that. Bess is too much adiposed, and Belle—"

"Well?"

"She is too un-adiposed, if you like it better. Not to put to fine a point upon it, as Mr. Snagsby used to say—she's too thin."

"Not faults in either of them beyond repair," commented Jack. "Cora is very keen about them. Thinks they're the best ever. She is very much interested in them."

"How about Jack?" teased Ed. "He might have a perfectly pardonable interest in being Interested in the twins—solely on his sister's account, however—solely an the part of his sister."

"Um!" murmured Jack. "That's neither here nor there. To carry it a little further, and still discussing the twins, there is Ed Foster, who is always at college when he is not fishing. He has money to burn, and so he's going to set fire to some of it by entrusting it to the New City Bank."

"Not quite money to burn," said Ed as he carefully threw out the baited hook again. "I've about twenty thousand dollars that came from father's estate, and it is stipulated that it must be most carefully secured. I think the new bank a good investment. But as for that being a drawing-card in my favor, why look to yourself. Here's Jack Kimball," went on Ed, "the best musician at Exmouth. The girls' pet, and, altogether, a very nice boy. I believe that's all—no, hold on. I never said a word about your weakness for chicken potpie, although you did appropriate my dish the last day at college."

"I was hungry," pleaded Jack. "But I thank you for your considerate description. Do you think that you now have the Chelton folks to rights?"

"We haven't touched on Walter Pennington. He seems to be the whole thing with the girls," and Ed did not try to disguise his tone of sarcasm.

"Oh, yes—Walter," said Jack. "Oh, Walter's all right. He seems to have more time to spend fussing around the girls than the rest of us have."

"Is that it?" asked Ed. "I thought it was the other way about. That the girls had more time for Walter than for the rest of us."

"I don't pretend to understand you," remarked Jack, pulling up quickly and looking in disgust at his empty hook. "But if you want anything—why, go in and win, as Priscilla said to John Alden. You can beat Walter—you're handsomer."

"Drop that!" cried Ed, looking for a clod of earth to throw at Jack. Then he ran his fingers through his thick, black hair. He was handsome, but he did not like it "cast up to him."

"Oh, I don't know," he murmured after a pause. "Walter has a way with him. Girls 'perfectly love' that uncertain shade of hair. It's capable of being made over to suit—"

"Knocking!" cried Jack. "You're knocking! I'll tell Walter. You called him a—"

"A first-rate chap, and I mean it!" insisted Ed warmly. "That's just what I think of Walter Pennington."

"Well, you know what I've always thought of him," and Jack was equally enthusiastic. "Walter is the kind of a fellow that will keep without canning."

"Meaning some others won't—such as Sid, for example?"

"Well, he's very `close' sometimes, so to speak. At least very hard to understand. But let's talk about something else. When do you go over to the bank, to stand and deliver your good cash, bonds and securities for their stock?"

"This very afternoon, may it please the court. And, by the same token, I should be getting home now. Hope we won't meet anyone, or they might ask, as Sid did, if I'd been clamming. I can't seem to keep out of the mud."

They gathered up their fishing paraphernalia and walked out to the highway.

"Are you and your money going over in the machine?" asked Jack.

"Certainly. Why not? Henry Porter is going to loan me his runabout."

"Oh, I suppose it's all right, but it's a lot of money to carry with you alone—twenty thousand dollars."

"And to hear you talk I might suspect that you had designs on it. I guess I'll get over to New City with it safe and sound. I hardly think I need a bodyguard."

"Humph! Maybe not. I guess you'll be all right."

"Your sister seems much interested in motoring," remarked Ed as they trudged along.

"Oh, yes, sis is just wild about it. She learned to run my car, and then began teasing for one of her own. We a were waiting for her seventeenth birthday to give it to her—mother and I—"

"Oh, I suppose you paid for part of it," remarked Ed with a laugh.

"No; but I ran it up from the garage for her. It's a fine, up-to-date car, and now that sis has it she's as happy as a kitten lapping up sweet cream."

"And she's as plucky as—um—what shall I say? I never saw any one manage a car better than she did the day the brake wouldn't work and they nearly ran into the train. I declare, when I saw her dive through that gap in the fence and steer toward me through the pond, I felt like yelling. I was almost frozen stiff. Couldn't do a thing but look on."

"And sis thawed you out with a mud bath," said Jack. "Oh, Cora's all right, even if I am her brother."

"She certainly is a star, if I may be pardoned the expression. Well, here's where I'm going to leave you. I've got to stop at the post-office. People have gotten into the habit lately, and a mean habit it is, of mailing me bills about the first of the month. One would think they might let a fellow have a vacation from that sort of thing once in a while."

"Oh, I get mine, too. And this month they're rather heavier than usual, as it's Cora's birthday."

"There's Sid," suddenly remarked Ed, pointing down the road to where Sidney Wilcox was coming around a turn, walking slowly.

"Yes, and I guess he gets his bills, too."

"Likely," admitted Ed. "He seems to have one now, and it doesn't appear to please him," for Sid was intently studying a sheet of paper as he walked along. He turned back and looked up the road.

"Who's he looking for?"' asked Jack.

"Give it up. No, I don't, either. There she is. It's Ida Giles."

Sidney waited for the girl to come up to him. Then he put the sheet of paper in his pocket, and the two walked along together until they came abreast of Ed and Jack. Sid nodded, which salutation was returned by the two fishermen. Ida made a slight motion with her head, which might or might not have been taken for a bow. Then the two passed on.

"My, but they're rushing it pretty fast!" commented Jack.

"Oh, Sid owns a nice little car—built for two," spoke Ed. "That makes it worth while for her."

"Yes, Ida does get in a lot of runs."

Jack turned to look at the girl. She was rather becomingly dressed in a dark-blue gingham sailor suit. Her red hair seemed fairly to blaze in the summer sunlight. Her companion slouched along in that indifferent way common to many youths of neutral temperaments—nothing much decided about them save their dislike for hard facts.

Ed and Jack had now reached the beginning of the sidewalk leading into town. They noticed a torn envelope lying on the flags. It was, as they could see, addressed to Sidney Wilcox, and in one corner was the imprint of an auto firm, which made the style of car that Sid drove. The fishermen smiled at each other, but made no remark. Perhaps the envelope had contained a bill.

"I may take a spin out on the road this afternoon," said Jack at parting. "Cora and the twins are going out, and we have promised to trail along after them."

"We?" questioned Ed.

"Yes. Walter and I, of course."

"Oh, of course—Walter."

"Jealous!" called Jack. "But cheer up. Perhaps we shall meet' you, and you'll have a chance."

"Oh, I'll be too busy with the cash, I'm afraid. But, at any rate, give my regards to your sister."

"Surest thing you know. How about the twins?"

"Well—er—never mind."

"All right. Say, Ed, come over to dinner some night. I want mother to meet you."

"All right, I will."

Ed turned away. He seemed unusually thoughtful. Was it Jack's remark about carrying so much money, unprotected, along the highway that caused it? It was a large sum—twenty thousand dollars. But he was strong enough to take care of himself. Besides, he would have his revolver with him. He decided on this, though at first it had not occurred to him.

Then he laughed aloud at his worriment and his prospective precautions. Who ever heard of any one being robbed on the road from Chelton to New City?

CHAPTER Y

AN IMPROMPTU RACE

"All ready!"

It was Cora who spoke. She and her chums, the Robinson twins, and a fourth girl, were about to start out for the afternoon run Jack had mentioned. The fourth girl was Mary Downs, a little millinery model and helper, to whom Cora had promised a ride in the new car. It was Mary's initial spin, and, as Cora cranked up, the young girl, with the queer, deep-set eyes, and the long, oval face so dear to the hearts of model-hunters, fairly quivered with anticipation.

"Are you all right, Mary?" asked Cora with a reassuring smile.

"Oh, yes," replied the girl with a happy little laugh. "This is—just glorious!"

"Wait just a minute," begged Bess. "I want to tie my hat on more securely. I do hope we get our auto bonnets soon."

"Madam said they would be finished to-day," remarked Mary. "They are very pretty, I think." Madam Julia was Mary's employer.

"Chug! chug!" sounded from the motor as it speeded up, momentarily, drowning all conversation. Then, as Cora climbed in and adjusted the throttle and shifted the spark lever, she let in the clutch, and the car rolled gently away.

"Where were the boys to meet us?" asked Belle.

"At the turnpike junction," replied Cora as she deftly threw in the high speed gear, and that without the terrific grinding of the cogs that betrays the inexperienced hand. The Whirlwind leaped forward, and the girls clutched their hats. "Jack promised he wouldn't be a minute late," went on Cora as she turned out to avoid a rut.

"Jack usually is on time," murmured Isabel. She almost lisped, yet the more you heard it the more you thought it was but a pretty little catch in her voice—in the accent—after the manner of babies, who seem to defer all they have to say to their listener. Every one loved Isabel.

"Oh, you think so, do you?" asked her sister. "Jack never makes any mistakes apparent to Belle," she added with an arch glance at Cora, with whom she was riding on the front seat.

"Never mind," murmured Belle.

Mary listened to the talk with evident pleasure. She was not accustomed to this sort of perfectly frank jokes.

"There they are!" suddenly cried Cora as the Get There swerved into sight around the corner.

Jack, who was at the wheel of his car, with Walter beside him, swung in close to his sister's machine.

"All right?" asked Jack, looking critically at Cora as she slowed up the big car, and noting her firm grip of the steering wheel.

"Fine and dandy!" exclaimed the girl, with the expression that makes that sort of slang a parody rather than a convenience.

"And if there aren't Sid and Ida!" exclaimed Belle. "Seems to me we run into them wherever we go."

"As long as it's only metaphorically and not mechanically speaking, it's all right," observed Walter.

The yellow Streak glided smoothly along.

"Quite a parade," remarked Jack.

"Let's make it a race," suggested Cora, her dark eyes flashing in anticipation.

Jack glanced at Walter. The relations between him and Sid were rather strained. As for Ida—well, Ida was credited with "running after Walter," and the sentiment of lads toward such girls is too well known to need describing.

"Oh, yes! Do let us race!" chimed in Bess. "It would be such fun!"

"All right," agreed Jack. "That is, if Sid is, willing."

"Will you race, Sidney?" called Cora, before the occupants of the yellow car had had time to greet the others.

"Yes, certainly," he assented. "I would like nothing better."

"Then we'll have to handicap the girls," suggested Walter. "They have by far the fastest machine."

"But it's brand new," objected Cora, "and isn't tuned up yet, as the two runabouts are. Besides, look who we are—girls."

33

"Very charming ones, I'm sure," said Sid quickly, but, somehow, his voice did not ring true.

"Handicap," spoke Walter. "I suppose it's right, but you see —er—we fellows could—" He was floundering about for a way of saying that the girls should not be penalized by giving the drivers of the two runabouts a start. For, in spite of their small size and less power the runabouts were speedy cars. It seemed as if Walter did not want to take the obviously fair advantage due him.

"Oh, no," declared Cora. "We'll let you handicap us all you wish. We are willing to test the Whirlwind on its merits."

"I should think so," sneered Ida, and then she turned disdainfully away, as if the landscape held more of interest for her than did the details of a race.

"Who is that forward girl?" asked quiet Mary of Bess.

"Ida Giles," was the whispered reply.

"She looked at me as if I did not belong in a motor car," went on the little milliner, with that quick perception acquired by business experience.

"Well, she doesn't belong in the one she's in," retorted Bess kindly. "I guess you imagine she meant something like that. Ida is not really mean. She is merely thoughtless."

"That's the very meanest kind of meanness," insisted Mary, "for, when folks do a thing through thoughtlessness they do not know enough to be careful next time."

Bess smiled to assure Mary that the milliner's model was on an equal footing with the girls in the Whirlwind, at all events.

"Line up!" called Jack. "Get ready for the race. We'll not insist on a handicap for you, Cora."

Sid sent his car directly to the middle of the road, the very best place.

"Better let the touring car go there," suggested Walter in as even a tone as he could command. "It will need lots of room, and the road's not very wide."

"That's right," added Jack. "A runabout can go on either side, then."

"I don't know," began Sid. "Cora ought to beat, and yet with two fellows driving against her—"

34

"Oh, if it's a matter of girls," almost sneered Ida, "I'll drive the Streak."

"Good idea!" hurriedly spoke Jack. "That will `make the match even. Suppose we take a girl to drive our car, Walter?"

Walter glanced rather ruefully at his companion.

"Why—er—yes," he drawled. "Suppose we take—"

"Bess," finished Jack, quickly. "She knows considerable about a car, and she's driven this one."

Somehow, the idea of having Bess as a rival to Ida suggested fun to Jack.

"Now we have it," went on Cora's brother, as Bess alighted from the Whirlwind and entered the Get There. "Are we all ready?"

"Where's Walter going?" asked Cora, for he had given up his seat to Jack, who moved to make room for Bess. Mary, Cora and Belle were in the touring car.

"I guess I'd better get into the big machine,", decided Walter. "Three such pretty girls in it all alone are an unequal division of beauty and talent—the last for myself, of course."

He moved toward the Whirlwind. Ida frowned. She had rather hoped to have matters so arranged that Walter would be with her. Cora saw the frown and laughed merrily as Walter slipped into the seat beside her.

"I suppose you think you are going to do the mascoting for this car," she said.

"At your service, mademoiselle," replied Walter, trying to bow, a politeness rather difficult of accomplishment in a small seat. "Do anything you like, but don't run me into the ditch. My watch is deadly afraid of ditches."

Then Cora introduced Mary, the little model blushing refreshingly.

Walter made a mental note of Mary's eyes, and the soft tints, like the bloom of a peach, in her cheeks. The two other girls were not slow to observe his interest. It was odd, thought Cora, how boys go in for the romantic sort—and models!

"All ready?" called Jack again.

Ida shook her head. She looked critically at the clutch lever, from her seat at the wheel, which Sid had relinquished to her. The lever was not properly adjusted, and she called her companion's attention to it.

Sid shifted it, and then Walter called from his seat beside Cora.

"All ready here!"

"It's about time," murmured Jack, jokingly.

The cars, which had been cranked, were "chug-chugging" away, and vibrating with the speed of the unleashed motors. Three clutch pedals were released, and the three cars moved forward. There was a grinding of gears, as Ida threw in a higher speed. Her hand and ear were not quite true, but to the surprise of the others her car darted ahead. It was speedier than had been thought.

It was a beautifully clear road, and the machines were now fairly flying along it. Bess clung desperately to the wooden rim of the steering wheel of Jack's car.

"Keep her straight," he cautioned. "Don't work so hard at it. An auto is like a horse—a light, firm touch is what it needs."

"Um!" murmured Bess. She was afraid to open her mouth lest she should lose her breath in the wind.

"Look out for that wagon!" Walter suddenly called to Cora.

A clumsy vehicle was some distance in advance, and seemed to be standing still, so slow was the movement. Ida was nearer to it than the others, and as she passed it she swung safely to one side, giving several disconcerting blasts on the horn as she did so. She was proving herself a good driver.

Somehow Bess had managed to distance the big car and had swung to second place. Cora thought she had her machine going at full speed, but either it had not "warmed up" yet, or she was not properly feeding the gasolene, and had not correctly adjusted the sparking device.

Just as Cora was about to pass the wagon, which feat Bess had now safely negotiated, the old man driving it seemed to awaken from a nap. He appeared to remember something he had forgotten and pulled his horses to one side—the wrong side—toward Cora's car, which was rushing right at him! The Whirlwind was almost upon the wagon!

"Mercy!" screamed. Mary. "We'll be smashed!"

"Steady!" called Cora, though her face went white.

Walter reached over, as if to take the wheel from the girl. She stopped him by a shake of her head, and then braced herself for what was coming. She screamed at the top of her fresh, clear voice:

"Stop! stop! Don't turn! stop!"

The farmer heard just in time. He fairly pulled the horses back on their haunches, and the wagon came to a stop. There was barely room for the auto to get past, but Cora managed it.

"Oh!" sighed Mary in thankfulness. "Wasn't that awful?"

"A narrow escape," assented Isabel. "But not as bad as the other one was. You should have seen that! We're safe now."

The Whirlwind careened along the road, from the shelving gutter back into the middle of the highway.

"Why didn't you let me take the wheel?" asked Walter, looking at Cora in a strange sort of way.

"I couldn't seem to let go," she said with a nervous little laugh. "I knew, of course, that you could run it more safely than I could, but somehow I couldn't seem to let go. My fingers appeared to be glued to the wheel."

"I certainly could not have done better," admitted Walter. "But I thought I might help you. Look at Ida, though! She is going like grim death."

"If she doesn't encounter another farmer she may be all right," said Cora. "But I wonder why I don't go faster. Oh, no wonder. I'm on second speed. I forgot to throw in the high gear. Here it goes. Now watch me pass them."

She advanced the lever, and the car shot forward. It was going at a greatly increased speed, and easily passed Bess and Jack.

"Here's where we leave you," called Cora.

"It's about time," replied Jack. "I thought something was wrong with you.

"Third gear," answered Cora. "Forgot I had it." Her voice floated back on the wind.

With a merry shout she turned on more gasolene and advanced the spark. She was almost up to Ida.

The race was to end at a bridge, which was only a few rods ahead.

"Careful," cautioned Walter to the fair driver beside him. She was making some rather reckless curves.

"I'm all right," declared Cora.

"I'm sure we'll win," exclaimed Mary.

The Whirlwind was now close to Sid's car. He heard it coming and looked around. Then he caught the steering wheel from Ida, leaning over to reach it.

"Foul!" shouted Walter. "That's not allowed!"

"Never mind!" panted Cora. "I'm not afraid to let him steer. I can beat him!"

Jack stood up in his machine. He was angry, and showed it in his face.

"Stop, sis," he called to Cora. "The race is yours. Don't pass him."

"She can't!" retorted Sid.

"Oh, I'm afraid!" gasped Bess, beside Jack. "He's steering right in front of her to cut her off. He won't turn out."

Then, as if realizing that the race would be counted lost to them for Sid's violation of the rules, Ida tried to displace the hands of her, companion from the wheel.

"Let me steer"' she exclaimed. "I want to! Let me, Sid!"

"No!" he answered angrily. "I'm going to run it now."

The car was swaying from side to side because of the erratic motion imparted to it, due to the struggle between Sid and Ida to gain possession of the wooden circlet.

"Let me take it! I want to beat her!" spoke Ida in a tense whisper, and Sid, with a queer look at her, nodded.

He released his grip of the wheel, and again Ida took it in a firm grasp. But the change was not skillfully enough made, and the next moment the Streak cut diagonally across the road, right in front of the Whirlwind.

"Oh!" screamed Cora, in spite of herself, and Bess and Mary added their frightened cries. Cora swung the wheel as far to the right as it would go. There was a grinding sound as she threw on the emergency brake, and the powerful clutch of it held the rear wheels in so firm a grip that the big rubber tires fairly slid along the road.

"Sid," cried Ida, "they'll collide with us! Do something! Do it quick!"

He stood up and tried to take Ida's hands from the wheel again, but she seemed to have lost her head. The big car was still careening toward them, though the brakes were slowing it up. Then Ida, with a flash of instinct, did the only thing possible. Instead of putting on brakes and trying to stop, she pressed the accelerator pedal, and the little car shot forward at a momentarily increased speed. Between them Ida and Sid managed to steer it into a ditch, and brought up with a crash against a fence, splintering the rails. Ida, with more force than she thought she possessed, jammed on the brakes, and the Streak, with a groan and a jar, came to a stop.

Then there came a jolt, a ripping sound, and Cora's big, four-cylindered machine banged into the Streak, for, in spite of all Cora and Walter could do, the Whirlwind could not be stopped in time.

But, fortunately, the damage to the large car was not great, for as she saw that a collision was inevitable, Cora had quickly shifted the wheel, and but a glancing blow had been struck. A mud guard was torn from the Whirlwind. Only Cora's plucky driving, and her emergency stop, had prevented a worse accident.

"Well," remarked Sid in a strange voice, "we're alive, at any rate."

"Yes," added Bess sharply, "and no thanks to somebody, either."

"If you mean me—" began Sid, the color flaming into his face.

"Look at your radiator!" suddenly exclaimed Walter. "It's sprung a leak!"

A stream of water, trickling down from the front of the Streak testified to this. A piece of the broken fence rail had jammed into the radiator, puncturing several coils and bending others out of place.

"No more go in her," observed Sid ruefully. "We'll have to be towed back home."

"Is your car damaged much, Cora?" asked Walter, for the girl had leaped out and was critically examining the auto.

"Only the mud guard," she replied as she reached up to the steering wheel, touched the levers and shut off the engine.

CHAPTER VI

GETTING A TOW

For a few minutes every one seemed to be talking at once, and there was considerable confusion. Sid and Ida came in for a number of rather angry glances, for the mishap seemed to be due entirely to their thoughtless conduct, and that their runabout had been the most damaged did not appear to lessen their offense.

Walter took the wheel of the Whirlwind, which Cora gladly relinquished to him, and soon had the car out of the ditch and upon the highway. The Streak, of course, could not move under its own power for more than a short distance, as the water had all leaked out of the radiator, and, there being none to cool the cylinders, to operate it was to invite disaster. Jack and Bess had alighted from the Get There. Jack was very angry.

"Nice way to race!" he exclaimed. "I've got a good mind to—do something to you, Sid Wilcox!"

"Oh, you have, eh?" sneered Sid. "Well, I don't know but what I might like to take it out of you for your sister cutting so close across my course. I guess I'm the one to get mad,"

"You sneak! She did nothing of the sort!" cried Jack.

"Oh, Jack! Please don't!" begged his sister. "If it was my fault, I'm ready to apologize."

"Your fault!" exclaimed Walter. "It wasn't your fault at all. It was—er—well, Sid and Ida were to blame."

"That's the way it looked to me," declared Cora.

Ida stared at Jack's sister for a moment, and then, with an open sneer on her face, turned deliberately away.

"Oh, I'm so glad we escaped, anyhow!" ejaculated Mary Downes. Her voice attracted Sid's attention. He had not noticed the little work girl before. At first he appeared to scowl, and then he smiled most pleasantly. The action was not lost upon Belle, though Cora, puzzling over Ida's manner, had not seen it.

"Come on, get in, girls," called Walter from his seat in the touring car. "No use standing there in the sun."

"You've got to tow me," ordered Sid in a peremptory manner.

"Got to?" repeated Walter, with a curious inflection.

"Hush!" whispered Cora. "Let's do it, Walter. Jack is so angry at him that I'm afraid something will happen."

"Very well. Just as you say," replied Walter gallantly.

Jack turned away in disgust. He was evidently trying hard to keep his temper under control.

"That he and Ida should deliberately endanger the lives of several people, to say nothing of their own risk, seems past belief," Jack murmured to Walter. "I've a good mind to teach him a much-deserved lesson. We ought to leave him to walk home."

"Oh, I do dislike rows!" exclaimed Cora, and she whispered in Jack's ear: "Don't bother with him, Bud. He isn't worth it."

"You're right about that," was the response, and the lad looked affectionately at his sister. She had gotten over the momentary fright, and there was now a pretty flush on her face. "I'll overlook it this time, sis," went on Jack. "Perhaps he'll get his lesson later—without me having to give it to him."

"Aren't some of you going to tow me?" asked Sid rather disconsolately. "I can't run my car the way it is."

"Don't ask any favors of them," Cora heard Ida whisper to Sid. "We'll walk."

"I will not," he answered sharply. "I'm not going to leave my car here. Will you give me a tow, Cora?" he asked. "Seeing that you made me smash—"

"She did not!" cried Jack. "And if you say so you're—"

"Jack!" exclaimed his sister.

"Well, he knows it was his own fault," concluded Jack, not wishing to accuse Ida.

Sid looked a bit worried.

"We'll tow you," said Cora simply.

"Thank you," responded Sid.

"Got a rope?" asked Walter.

41

"Here's one," answered the owner of the Streak, producing a strong rope from the rear of his runabout.

"Looks as if you were in the habit of getting towed," remarked Walter.

"Yes. I've had bad luck with this car."

Sid and Walter were soon busy arranging the two cars, so that the big auto would tow the disabled one.

"I want the boys to separate," whispered Cora to Bess. "I'm so Afraid Jack and Sid will quarrel."

"Not if they keep as far apart as they are now," was the answer, for Jack had gotten back into his own car, and was looking on. Ida, too, seemed to keep herself at a distance from the other girls.

"Well, I guess that will hold," remarked Walter as he put the last knot in the rope.

"Here comes Ed Foster!" suddenly exclaimed Jack as the puffing of an auto was heard and a machine came in sight. "Now I guess we're all here. Hello, Ed!"

"Hello, yourself," replied Ed. "Well, what's up now? Somebody turned turtle?"

"No, but somebody's turned—" began Jack, on the point of saying something uncomplimentary about Sid, but Cora interrupted him.

"We had a race, and this is how I—that is, we—won it," she said with a laugh.

Ed stepped out of his car and walked to where Sid's silent machine stood.

"Radiator, eh?" he questioned. "A bad break."

"That's what. Cora collided with me—but it was partly my fault," added Sid quickly for jack's benefit.

"And look at my nice, new mud guard," spoke Cora. "See how it hangs down, like a dog's broken leg. Isn't it a shame? I guess we'll have to tear it off, so we can run."

"Let me look at it," suggested Ed. "Maybe I can spring it back into place."

"I never thought of that,"—remarked Walter.

Ed was searching in his tool-box, and presently drew out some strong string.

"I never go without a bit of cord, a knife and some pins for just such emergencies as these," he said with a laugh. "I never know when I may be shipwrecked on a desert island."

Ed skillfully sprung the guard back, and as one of the rivets was torn out, he lashed the protector into place. It was only a temporary repair, but it would protect the occupants of the car from a shower of dust or mud.

"There," said Ed finally. "I guess that will answer. The road ahead is pretty muddy. Too much moisture from a sprinkling-cart, I guess. I caught some of it."

Cora turned to see if everything was in readiness for a start, and was surprised to find Mary in close conversation with Ida. Both girls and Sid were in a group an the other side of the Whirlwind. And another thing Cora noticed was that the faces of both Ida and Mary were unusually flushed.

"That's rather odd—that Mary and Ida should get so chummy," murmured Cora. "Sid must have introduced them to each other:"

A moment later Ida looked over, and seeing Cora watching her, she quickly turned away and walked over to where Ed was locking up his toolbox. She placed her hand on the seat of his small auto and began talking to him.

"I hear you are going into business," Cora heard Ida say.

"Well, not exactly business," replied Ed. "I'm going to have some interest in the bank at New City."

"Oh, yes. I heard about it."

"Say, Ed, have you all that—" began Jack, and then he stopped quickly. He had been on the point of asking Ed if he had with him the twenty thousand dollars in cash and negotiable securities, but he quickly reflected that such a question was not a proper one to ask on a public road.

"Got what?" inquired Ed with a laugh, but at the same time Cora saw him frown slightly at her brother.

"I meant to say, have you any of those fish with you that we caught last time?" asked Jack, laughing rather uneasily.

"Yes, I have them," replied Ed, which was his way of replying to Jack's implied question.

"Going over to New City?" asked Sid, coming around from an inspection of the broken radiator.

"Yes; I've some business over there, and as it's getting late I'll have to hurry. I'll bid you all good-by. Hope you get safely home."

Ed jumped into his car, which he had quickly cranked up, and called a general farewell.

"So long," answered Jack.

"Come on," called Walter, as Ed's car puffed out of sight. "We'll have a load to pull now, Cora."

"Perhaps I had better get in with Jack and Bess," remarked Belle. "We can manage it—if we squeeze some."

Then she blushed, and everybody laughed.

"The more the merrier," replied Jack. "I think it will be a good idea, though. We'll get home quicker than Cora and her tow will."

Belle climbed into the Get There. This left Cora alone with Walter in the big car. Ida and Sid stood on the ground, apparently waiting for an invitation to get in somewhere.

"I'll have to steer my car," said Sid. "You had better get in Cora's machine, Ida, for it's no fun riding in a towed auto."

"Yes, do come in here," said Cora quickly, but Ida hung back and looked miserably unhappy.

"Come on," and Walter added his invitation. "I'm going to be the 'shuffler,' and I may as well have something worth while to 'shuffle' while I'm at it."

Ida smiled at this. It was evident that she could not resist after this appeal—especially as it came from Walter, who found much favor in her eyes.

Ida climbed into the big car nimbly enough, and sat on the thick cushions in the roomy tonneau beside Mary.

"I guess she'd rather be in front," remarked Bess in a whisper to Belle, but she took care that Jack should not hear.

Walter started Cora's car off, and Sid's followed, with himself at the wheel, looking very glum. Jack brought up in the rear with the pretty twins.

The Whirlwind easily towed the weight of the disabled runabout, and the autoists were soon approaching town.

"Let me out at the post-office, please," begged Mary of Cora, as they rolled through the village streets. "I had better not let madam see me out riding."

"Why, she gave you permission, didn't she?" asked Cora in surprise.

"But I would rather get out here," insisted Mary, not answering the question directly.

"If you'll cast me loose, I'll run my machine in this shop," suddenly called Sid, as they passed a rather tumble-down shack on a side street.

"But you're not going to let old Smith tinker with it, are you?" asked Walter.

"Oh, I don't know what I'll do with it!" snapped Sid. "May as well leave it here as anywhere else."

Smith's place was a second-rate blacksmith shop, while at Chelton Center, a little farther on, there was a fine garage—Newton's—the one at which Cora and the twins had met the handsome machinist.

"Why don't you take it to Newton's?" asked Cora. "We'll go there with you. I—er—, I know the machinist there."

"I prefer to leave it here," said Sid shortly. "Stop, please, and I'll loosen the rope."

"Oh!" exclaimed Cora shortly. She could not understand Sid. Walter stopped her car, and before it had come to a full halt Sid was detaching the tow rope. Mary took this chance to alight from the Whirlwind, as they were not far from the post-office, and Ida followed her. Sid cranked up for the short run into the blacksmith shop. Ida and Mary were walking down the street together.

"Go ahead!" Sid called to Walter.

"Oh, you're welcome," replied Walter sarcastically. "Not the least trouble, thank you. Glad at any time—"

Sid shot at him an angry glance over his shoulder.

"I'd like to know who had a better right to haul me out of the ditch?" he said sneeringly.

Jack, with the twins, had run on. As Walter started Cora's machine off again, they saw a man coming out of the smithy. He helped Sid push the car in, and then stood talking with him in a friendly sort of fashion. The man's clothing was unkempt, and his general appearance anything but prepossessing.

"Who's that?" asked Cora.

"Him, you mean?" inquired Walter. "Oh, that's Lem Gildy. Or just plain Lem, if you like that better."

"What does he do?"

"Nothing. Easily said. Yet I've heard it remarked that he'd do anything for money."

"Curious that Sid should be on such friendly terms with such a character."

"Rather," remarked Walter, and he turned to see Sid pointing at the big car, while Lem Gildy was nodding his head as if assenting to something.

CHAPTER VII

TWENTY THOUSAND DOLLARS LOST

Edward Foster, as he ran his machine along the country road toward New City, where he was to transact his business at the bank, was thinking of many things. And not all of them were connected with the large sum of money and the bonds which he was to exchange for stock. A certain bright-eyed girl figured largely in his reveries.

"Guess I'd better put on a little more speed," he said to himself. "It's going to take some time to get this all straightened out, and I don't like to have such a large sum with me on the road."

He speeded up his car, and was soon on the outskirts of the city, where he had to go slower, threading his way in and out among many vehicles.

He reached the bank shortly before noon, was greeted by the president and the secretary, who were expecting him, and was shown into a private office.

"Well, we have the stock all ready for you," said the president genially. It was not every day that his bank disposed of such a large block. "I trust you will find it a good investment."

"I believe I will," replied Ed as he reached his hand in his inner pocket to take out the wallet that contained the money and bonds. "I looked into—"

He stopped suddenly. A blank look came over his face. Hurriedly he felt in another pocket. Then he began a rapid search through his clothes.

"What's the matter?" asked the secretary. "Did you mislay your valuables?"

"Yes—no—I don't see—" murmured Ed. All the while he was making a frantic search. His face paled. The bank officials looked anxiously on.

"Can't you find it?" inquired the president.

"I've either lost my wallet,—or it's been stolen!" burst out Ed desperately.

"How could it have been stolen?" asked the secretary.

"I don't know," was the answer. "I don't see how it could have been, as, from the time it was in my pocket until now, I did not leave my auto—"

He stopped quickly. The memory of the scene alongside the road, where the machines had collided, came back to him with vivid distinctness. He had alighted there, and—

He pursued his reflections no further, but hurriedly got up from the chair.

"I must go back at once," he said. "I will make a search. I think I know where the loss may have taken place."

"Or the theft," suggested the president.

"No," said Ed slowly, "I don't believe it was a theft."

"Shall we send for a detective? Will you take one of our porters or a watchman with you?" asked the secretary.

"No; I think I'll make a search myself, first, thank you. And please don't tell the police—yet. I may have dropped it. I'll let you know as soon—as soon as I go to a certain place and look. There is time enough to notify the authorities afterward. I'll telephone you if I don't find it, and then I'll tell the police in Chelton. But I must hurry."

"Yes; you had better lose no time," advised the president.

"The thief—if there, was one—could easily dispose of those securities. As for the money—?"

"He would have no trouble in spending that," finished Ed. "Yes, I'll go back at once."

He hurried out to his auto, and was soon speeding back over the road on which he had come. He reached the spot where the auto collision had occurred, and where he had helped fix Cora's machine. Jumping from the car he looked carefully over the ground, but could find no trace of the missing wallet, containing the equivalent of twenty thousand dollars.

"I must hurry to tell the police," he murmured as he urged his machine forward at top speed. A little later Cora and Walter, who had returned to Chelton, saw Ed standing on the steps of the police station.

"Why!" Cora exclaimed to Walter in some surprise, "I thought Ed was in New City, attending to that bank business."

"He ought to be," commented Walter. Then, noting Ed's white face, he added: "Something's happened!"

A moment later Jack, who had left the Robinson twins at their home, drove up in his runabout, and stopped it beside his sister's larger car. He, too, saw Ed Foster's white face.

"What's the matter, Ed?" he called quickly. "Are you hurt?"

"No," was the answer, and the voice was strained.

"But something has happened," insisted Cora as she alighted from her car and started up the steps of the police station.

"Yes," he said, and his voice trembled, "something has happened."

"What?" asked Jack.

"I've lost twenty thousand dollars—or—else it has been stolen!"

"Twenty thousand dollars!" cried Jack. "The money you were taking to the bank?"

Ed nodded.

"Where?" was Jack's next question.

"That's what I don't know. If I did I'd go get it."

"But if it was stolen—" began Cora.

"The thief is far enough away from here now," finished Ed, trying to smile. "However, I think I lost it near where the collision took place. I just came from there to report the matter to the police."

"But how could you lose it?" asked Cora, taking off her heavy driving gloves and fanning her face with them.

"I don't know, unless when I leaned over to fix the mud guard of your auto the wallet may have slipped from my pocket. But I've looked every inch about that spot," and then Ed related how he had come to miss the money and securities.

"Oh, we must go back and help you look!" exclaimed Cora quickly. "Of course we will, won't we, Jack—Walter?"

"Sure," replied her brother, and Walter gravely nodded. He was trying to recall every incident of the happenings after the collision.

"We'll go right away," went on Cora. "Crank up, Walter. Few persons go over that road in the afternoon, and maybe we can find it."

"Oh, I assure you that it's useless," declared Ed. "I am only waiting here to report the matter to Chief Jenkins, and then I'm going to telephone the officials at the bank in New City, as I promised I would."

"Can't you stop payment?" asked Jack.

"Not on the money, and not very easily on the negotiable securities. That's the unfortunate part of it. If it had been a check I could."

"Queer, I almost had a premonition that something might happen to that twenty thousand," said Jack slowly. "Though I suppose if I say that it makes it look bad for me," he added with a smile.

"Oh, no," Ed answered, seriously enough. "Of course not."

"Come on; let's hurry back," suggested Cora. She re-entered the car, which shook from the running of the ungeared motor that Walter had started for her.

"Really, Cora," began Ed, "it is useless for you to take the trouble to go back and hunt for it, though I'm sure it's very kind—"

"It's no trouble at all."

"But have you been home to dinner?" asked Ed.

"No. Walter and I stopped at a little wayside restaurant and had lunch. Come on, we'll hurry back to the place where the collision took place. I'm sure we'll find the wallet. I'm very lucky that way."

"Let me wish you the best of luck," said Ed with an attempt at gallantry. "I'd go with you, only I must give the chief all the particulars, in case it's stolen, you know. Then I must telephone to the bank."

"That's all right," put in Jack. "Go ahead. We'll make a hunt for that small fortune. Can I do anything for you here?"

"No, thanks. I think not. You are going to have a useless errand, though, I fear, but I appreciate what you are doing for me."

"Come on—hurry!" cried Cora, all impatient to be off, and then, when Walter climbed in beside her and Jack sent his car off, following the big machine of his sister, Ed disappeared behind the door of the police station.

CHAPTER VIII

A VAIN SEARCH

"Here's where the collision occurred!" exclaimed Cora a little later, when her car and Jack's, having been sent at a fast speed down the road, came to a halt, and she directed her brother's attention to the spot.

"No, this isn't it," objected Walter. "It's farther on. It's right near an old stump, don't you remember?"

"Oh, yes," answered Cora as she sent her car ahead again. "This is where we nearly ran into the wagon. I'm so excited I can't think straight."

"Well, be sure you steer straight!" cried Jack from the rear. "I don't want to run into you. Better let Walter take the wheel."

"Indeed, I'll do nothing of the sort!" cried Cora, laughing. "With all due respect to you, Walter, of course," she added with a bright look up into the face of her companion. "But don't you think I can manage my machine pretty well?"

"More than pretty and more than well," was her escort's reply. "Jack is a base defamer of your ability."

"Oh, you had to say that, Walt!" cried Jack, the irrepressible. "Push on. We want to get that money before some one walks off with it."

They were soon at the spot, where many tracks in the road showed that there the collision had taken place. Here was where Ed had alighted to fix Cora's car. His small machine had on a set of peculiar tires, and the impressions and indentations of the rubber shoes, which were new, were plainly, visible in the road.

Stopping their machines alongside the highway, the three young people began a careful search of the dusty stretch. They went over every inch of the ground, particularly in the vicinity of the place where Ed had stopped to fix the broken mud guard. But there was no sign of the pocketbook.

"Maybe it was dropped farther back," suggested Jack.

"Well, we'll try there," assented Cora, and for ten minutes they walked up and down the road, some distance back from the place where Ed had alighted.

"Now try farther on," was Walter's suggestion, and they did this.

51

But all to no purpose. They were not rewarded by the welcome sight of a brown leather wallet, bulging with riches.

"It's no use," said Jack.

"Oh, let's try a little longer," begged Cora.

"Well, if he dropped it before he got here, or after he left, we might as well make the entire trip to New City, and then reverse and go to Chelton," went on Jack. "And we can't look over every inch of all the distance."

"We can drive along slowly," was Cora's idea. "The wallet is so large that it could easily be seen. It's too bad we haven't Sid and Ida along to help hunt for it. And the Robinson girls, and Mary. The more eyes, the better. I'll go on to New City, if you'll make a search on the road from here to Chelton, Jack."

"Oh, I don't know as it would do any good."

"It won't do any harm," said Walter. "That is, if Cora isn't too tired."

"Oh, I should love to go. I can't get enough of my new car. Will you come, Walter?"

"Of course."

"Then, Jack, you go back to Chelton and keep a lookout on both sides of the road."

"Hard to do that with one pair of eyes," was her brother's reply. "I wish I had some one to ride with me. But go ahead; I'll do the best I can."

"It would be a good plan," assented Cora, "to have a person with you. If you could pick up some one—"

"Or run across somebody," added Jack with a grin.

"No, Jack, I'm serious. Don't joke. Even a stranger would do. Some man—"

"Here comes a man now!" exclaimed Walter as an individual came in sight around a bend in the road. The man was not very well dressed.

"I don't like his looks," said Jack in a low voice. "He seems like a tramp."

"I don't blame you for not liking his looks," interrupted Walter. "That's Lem Gildy."

"The man we saw talking to Sid when he ran his auto into the blacksmith shop?" asked Cora.

Walter nodded.

"Humph!" mused Jack. "I don't exactly fancy telling Lem Gildy about a pocketbook containing twenty thousand dollars lying alongside the road. He might not admit that he saw it if he happened to spy it while with me, and later on he might come back and pick it up."

"Well, don't tell him what you're looking for," suggested Cora with ready wit. "Just say it's—er—a—er—"

"Say it's a lady's pocketbook," put in Walter, "and then he'll know it's got everything in it but money. That's playing a safety with a vengeance."

"Oh, so that's your opinion of us, is it?" asked Cora quickly. "But, after all, Jack, I think it's the best plan to ask him to ride back with you, and have him watch one side of the road. Of course, he's rather dirty—I mean his clothes—and it's not nice to sit alongside of him, but—"

"Oh, I don't mind clean dirt," interrupted Jack. "It's only garden soil on Lem's clothes. He does odd jobs, you know."

"Not very often," added Walter. "But go ahead, Jack. He's coming nearer. I don't believe you can do better than ask him to ride back to Chelton with you. Needn't be too specific about what's in the pocketbook. But two pairs of eyes are better than one, you know."

"All right," assented Jack. "Here goes."

Lem Gildy was shuffling along the road. He was a particularly unprepossessing man, with a reddish growth of whiskers which he never seemed to take the trouble to shave off, and they stuck out like so many bristles in a half-worn toothbrush.

His teeth were yellow, and his habit of chewing tobacco was not to be commended. In short, he was a "shiftless" character, and nice persons had very little to do with him.

"Hello, Lem!" called Jack pleasantly.

"Hello," was the rather surly answer, and Lem shot a suspicious glance at Jack. It was not often that the young and wealthy Jack Kimball condescended to speak to Lem Gildy, and Lem realized it.

"Want a ride?" went on Jack, trying to make his voice sound natural.

"Don't look as if you was goin' my way," replied Lem with a grin. Then he turned his gaze on Cora, and the beautiful girl could not repress a shudder as she felt the bold glance of the man.

"Oh, I'm going to turn around," declared Jack. "I'm going back to Chelton. That's where you're headed for, I take it?"

"Sure. That's where I'm goin', and I'm tired, too. I've had a long walk this mornin', and—"

"Are you working in the blacksmith shop?" asked Walter quietly.

"No. What made you think that?" asked Lem quickly. "If you think—"

Then he stopped suddenly. An indignant look, that Lem had assumed, faded from his face. "No, I wasn't workin' there," he went on. "I—er—I just stopped in to see about gettin' a piece of iron."

"Well, do you want to ride back with me?" asked Jack, who wondered at Walter's question.

"That's what I do, if you're goin' my way."

"Yes, I'll turn around in a minute. Go ahead, Cora and Walter. Get back as soon as you can."

Jack cranked up his car, got in, and, running in a half circle, steered it to where Lem was standing.

"I ain't much in the habit of ridin' in these here kind of wagons," remarked Lem with a smirk. "I hope nothin' happens t' us."

"I guess nothing will. But, Lem, I'm not going to give you a ride for nothing," said Jack.

The man drew back suspiciously. He had expected something like this, his manner seemed to say.

"I ain't got any money," he whined.

"No, it's not money," went on Jack. "I only want you to help me look for something."

"Look for Suthin'?"

"Yes; along the road."

"What's the matter? Lose part of your autymobil?"

"No; it's a pocketbook—a wallet."

"A wallet?" exclaimed Lem, with such suddenness that Jack started.

"Yes," cried the lad. "You don't mean to say you found it?"

Lem seemed agitated. He shuffled his feet in the dust.

"Me find a pocketbook?" he said at length with a short laugh. "Well, I guess not. I ain't in the habit of findin' such things as that. What kind was it, and what was in it?"

"It was a long one of brown leather," replied Jack, describing Ed's pocketbook and ignoring the question of what was in it. "A friend of mine dropped it along here, and we're helping him hunt for it. My sister and Mr. Pennington are going to look in one direction, and you and I'll look in the other."

Jack tried to make his voice sound friendly, but it was difficult work.

"You'll look on one side of the road, and I'll keep watch on the other," he went on.

"All right; I'm agreeable," said Lem with a leer. "I don't believe we'll find it, though—I ain't never very lucky."

He got into the auto beside Jack, and the two started off slowly. Cora and Walter also started, and the search for the missing twenty thousand dollars was continued.

Jack and Lem did not talk much on the way back. Lem Gildy was not an accomplished conversationalist, and Jack was too anxious to find the wallet to care for the distraction of talk. Several times he thought he saw the pocketbook, but each time it was a flat stone or a clod of dirt that misled him.

They reached Chelton, and Lem asked to be set down in a secluded street.

"Why?" asked Jack curiously.

"Because if some of me chums saw me ridin' in a swell wagon like this they'd never speak to me again," and Lem grinned and showed all his yellow teeth. "I was afraid we wouldn't find that pocketbook," he added.

"Well, maybe Cora will," said Jack.

"Yes," said Lem slowly, "maybe she will—or some one else will."

His tone was so peculiar that Jack asked quickly:

"What do you mean, Lem?"

"Oh, nothin'," and the fellow assumed an injured air. "Only if a pocketbook is lost, some one's bound to find it, ain't they?"

"I suppose so," assented Jack, and as he drove his car through the streets of Chelton, after the unsuccessful search, he found himself vainly puzzling over Lem's strange manner.

Then, as he was turning a corner, Jack caught sight of Ed.

"Hey!" he called.

Ed turned. There was a momentary look of hope on his face.

"Did you—" he began.

Jack sadly shook his head.

CHAPTER IX

FINDING THE WALLET

"No luck, eh?" went on Ed as he approached Jack.

"No; that is, Lem and I didn't have any."

"Lem—do you mean to say Lem Gildy?"

"Now, don't get nervous. I didn't tell him it was your pocketbook that was lost. You see, I had to have some one keep watch on one side of the road while I looked on the other, and he was the only one available."

Then Jack related the details of the search.

"I'm glad Lem doesn't know about it," went on Ed. "I heard to-day that he and Sid Wilcox have been seen together several times lately, and I'm not quite ready to have my loss made public—especially to Sid."

"Maybe Cora and Walter will have better luck," suggested Jack hopefully. "We won't hear from them for some time, though. Did you 'phone to the bank in New City?"

"Yes. I told them I couldn't get any trace of the wallet here, and, as you know, I have already notified the Chelton police. They have been making a quiet search about town, but I fear it will be hopeless."

"The bank people didn't say it had been turned in there, by any chance, did they?"

"No such good fortune," and Ed laughed uneasily. "Well, I'm going home now to get a list of the bonds and their numbers, as well as the numbers of the big bills. The; police say they will want them when they send out a general alarm."

"But I thought you said you didn't want it generally known."

"I don't, until I have made a thorough search at home. It is barely possible that I took up the wrong wallet by mistake when I rushed out this morning. I have two that look exactly alike. I may have picked up the empty one, shoved it into my pocket, and lost that one. The one containing the bonds and cash may still be at my house. I am hurrying there to see. If I don't find it, the police are to send out a general alarm."

"I hope you find it."

"So do I. It means a big loss to me—almost my entire fortune gone. I don't know what I am going to do."

"Let's hope for the best," spoke Jack as cheerfully as possible, but there was a dubious look on his face as he watched Ed turn in the direction of his home.

But Ed found that he had made no mistake in the wallets. The empty one was safely in his room, but the one containing the twenty thousand dollars was—as he had feared—lost. He communicated this fact to the police, and soon the chief had ordered some handbills printed, describing the pocketbook and the contents, and offering a reward of five hundred dollars for the cash and bonds, Ed having agreed to pay this amount and ask no questions.

"Ha!" exclaimed Lem Gildy that night as one of the hastily printed bills came into his possession, "so this is the wallet they are lookin' for, eh? Twenty thousand dollars! But I knowed it all the while. As if Jack Kimball an' his sister could fool me! But I'll bleed him—that's what I'll do. I'll make him whack up—or—or I'lltell!" and Lem chuckled to himself, while there was a dangerous look on his mean face.

The search conducted by Cora and Walter was, as might be guessed, as unsuccessful as the one undertaken by Jack and Lem. Cora and Walter looked carefully over the whole length of the road to New City, but saw nothing of the wallet, and came back disconsolate in the auto.

"Poor Ed!" remarked Walter. "It's tough luck!"

"Yes, I wish we could have found it for him," agreed Cora as she skillfully drove the car through the Chelton streets at dusk. "I'm beginning to believe that it was stolen."

"I think so myself," added Walter. "But if he had it when he was fixing your car, and he missed it directly after he left our crowd—"

He hesitated a moment, then continued:

"Well, maybe he thinks that some of us may have—"

"Better not jump at conclusions," cautioned Cora, and at this Walter alighted near the street that led to his home.

"I won't," he promised Cora with a laugh as she sent the car ahead. She was anxious to reach home and learn the, details of Jack's search, though she and Walter knew, from an inquiry they had made at the bank in New City, that it had not been successful.

That night nothing was so important a topic of conversation in Chelton as the loss of the twenty thousand dollars. Speculation was rife, and opinion was equally divided on the question of whether it had been lost or stolen, or both, for that it might have been stolen after it was lost was possible.

Ed consulted some business friends, but they could give him little help. He was advised to hire private detectives, and said he would do so, in case the police of New City or Chelton could do nothing.

It was two days after the loss of the money and bonds that Cora, with her inseparable friends, the Robinson twins, and Walter, whom she had picked up on the road, were out for a ride. They took the turnpike, as it was the smoothest highway.

"We may meet Jack along here," said Cora as she turned out to avoid a large rock.

"Yes?"—asked Elizabeth, and she tried to keep down the eagerness in her voice.

"Yes; he's gone over to see about a concert his mandolin club is going to give, and he said he might bring a couple of the members back with him to stay a few days."

"College lads?" asked Bess with a laugh.

"Surely," replied Cora; "and charming ones, too, I gathered from Jack's talk."

"Must be some of the Never Sleep members," spoke Walter.

"Never Sleep members?" repeated Elizabeth.

"Yes; I belong. We call ourselves that because we used to be up at all hours. Some of the boys play in Jack's mandolin club."

"I hope we meet them!" exclaimed Bess frankly. "I'm dying for some music."

"Let me sing and save your life," proposed Walter.

"With pleasure," answered Bess, making a little gesture of surprise. "But I didn't know you sang."

"Only to save life," replied Waiter. "But," he added, "if I'm not mistaken that sounds like Jack's car."

"It is," declared Cora, who was getting to be an expert on the puffing sounds of autos. "There he is!" she exclaimed as Jack's runabout came in sight. "And it's pretty well crowded, too."

It was, for in the car, which would barely hold three, Jack had managed to squeeze four—three lads besides himself.

"Hello, sis!" he called as he caught sight of Cora. "You're just in time. Take one of these brutes out of here, will you? My springs are breaking."

"I'll go!" cried one lad as he caught sight of the Robinson twins.

"No, I saw 'em first!" exclaimed another.

"You did not! It's my turn to ride in a decent car," said the third.

"Now, just for that you will all three get in Cora's car, and I'll take the Misses Robinson in with me," declared Jack.

There was laughter at this, and Jack introduced his mandolin club friends to Cora and the twins.

"Seriously, though, sis, you'll have to take one or two of 'em," went on Jack. "Here, Diddick, you and Parks go in the big car. I want to talk to Youmans about the concert we're going to have."

Diddick and Parks gladly made the exchange into the larger car, while Youmans tried to look as if he liked to remain with Jack. But it was hard work to imagine it when he glanced across at the pretty twins and Cora.

"Hold on a minute," exclaimed Walter as he noticed that one of the rear tires of the touring car was flat. "We can't go on like this, Cora. That left tire will have to be pumped up."

"And you've got good muscles to do it, too, Walter," urged Diddick, smiling mischievously.

"We'll all help," volunteered Parks. "Come on!"

Diddick, Walter and Parks alighted. Walter stepped to the tool-box to get out the pump and the lifting-jack. As he was about to take them out he started back excitedly.

"Hurt yourself?" asked Cora, who was looking over the side of the car.

Walter shook his head. His face was strangely white as he spoke in a husky voice:

"The wallet! Ed Foster's wallet in the tool box—here—see!"

He held the pocketbook up to view.

"Where—where did you get it?" gasped Cora.

"In—in—your—tool—box!"

"What?"

The girl's voice was shrill, and there was a tremor in her tones. Cora fairly leaped out beside him. She was staring at the brown leather wallet the wallet that had contained the twenty thousand dollars.

"How on earth—" she began.

She reached out her hand for the pocketbook. Walter gave it to her. She raised up the flap, and uttered but a single word:

"Empty!"

The limp wallet fell from her hand to the ground. Cora's face turned strangely white, and she began swaying, as does a tree that a woodsman has nearly cut through.

A moment later the overwrought girl staggered and almost fell into Walter's arms.

CHAPTER X

SUSPICIONS

"Hello!" cried Jack, springing forward to his sister's aid. "I never knew Cora to do that before. Is she hurt, Walt?"

"No; only shocked, I guess."

"Help her into the car and put her on the rear seat," directed Belle.

"No; keep her head up," advised Bess.

"Somebody get water!" exclaimed Diddick, turning around in a circle to look for a spring.

Jack was rubbing his sister's hands, while Walter held her in a reclining position.

"There's a spring over by that tree," spoke Walter. "One of you get some water."

"I will—in my hat!" answered Parks, starting off on a run.

"Here's a cup," called Elizabeth, producing a collapsible one from a pocket in the tonneau of the touring car.

The lad took it, and came hurrying back with it half full of liquid, having spilled the rest on his hasty trip. Jack managed to get a little between Cora's lips, and it revived her. She opened her eyes, noted that Walter was holding her, and her face flushed slightly.

"I'm—I'm all right now," she declared as she tried to stand upright.

"Better get in the car and sit down," advised Jack.

She assented, and rather limply got into the tonneau of her machine. She drank some more water, and presently was herself again.

"How silly of me to nearly faint," she said with a wan smile. "But when I saw the pocketbook—empty—it was enough—"

"I should say so," interrupted Belle. "Who would ever have thought of finding it in your toolbox, Cora?"

The words seemed fraught with strange import.

"Was it really in the tool-box, Walter?" Cora asked.

"On top of the tire pump and the lifting-jack," replied Walter.

"And empty—that's the queer part of it," commented Belle. "I guess that's what shocked you as much as anything, Cora. Now, if it had had the twenty thousand dollars in it—"

"It's strange that the wallet should have been there—in my tool-box—at all," murmured Cora.

"It certainly is," added Jack. "What can it mean—to find it in Cora's car?"

"Is this the one Ed Foster lost?" asked Diddick. "We heard something about it."

"The same one," answered Walter as he picked the wallet from the road where it had fallen. "See, it has his name on it."

"I feel creepy—almost as if something supernatural had put it into my tool-box," said Cora in a curiously quiet voice.

"More likely some unnatural person did it," spoke Jack quickly. "Yet who in the world would do it? If I had seen—"

He stopped suddenly, leaving the sentence unfinished.

"And it was on top of the pump and jack," mused Cora, after a quick look at her brother. "I haven't used the pump since—let me see—"

"Since the day of the collision—the day when the pocketbook was lost," interrupted jack. "You pumped up a tire just before the race, so that the pocketbook must have been placed there right after the robbery."

"Or loss," added Walter. "Some one may have found the wallet, taken out the money and bonds, and then thrown the empty pocketbook away."

"That some one threw it in a curious place," remarked Elizabeth dryly.

"Indeed, they did," observed Cora. "It looks—"

She hesitated.

"Oh, you might as well say it—before some one else does," put in Jack. "It looks mighty suspicious, Cora."

There was a vindictive air about him. He seemed to challenge an accusation against his sister.

"I'm sure there was no need to say that," spoke Walter. "It may be a mere—er—"

"Coincidence," finished Cora.

"A queer coincidence," quoth Jack. "Incidentally, some one got the money, all right. We must hurry home and tell Ed."

"I wonder what he'll think?" asked Cora.

"What can he think?" demanded her brother. "Only that some one found or stole his wallet and threw the empty pocketbook into your tool-box."

"And I found it," added Walter. "Which might mean—"

He, too, hesitated.

"Well, what?" asked Jack.

"That I put it there, and only pretended to find it," finished Walter with a laugh.

"Nonsense!" exclaimed Cora. "But come, let's hurry back to Chelton. I want to be the first to tell Ed."

"Do you feel all right?" asked Jack anxiously.

"Oh, yes. Very well. I never fainted before, that I remember."

"Yes, you did. Once when you burned your hand on the stove," corrected Jack.

"Oh, that was a good while ago."

There was a period of silence.

"Well, as long as I started to pump up the tire I suppose I may as well finish," remarked Walter, as he took out the jack and raised the wheel.

It was rather a quiet company of young people who made their way back to Chelton in the two autos a little later. The gay members of the mandolin club had little to say, and when they did attempt a pleasantry the laughter was soon over. Every once in a while some one would refer to the discovery of the empty wallet.

"The next thing to find," remarked jack, with a trace of bitterness in his tones, "is the person with the cash and the bonds."

"Maybe they're in—the tool—box of your car," said Diddick jestingly. "It may run in the family—"

Then he was conscious that he had made rather a bad "break," and he subsided, while every one tried to talk at once to cover it up. Jack laughed uneasily, and Cora seemed annoyed.

One thought was running through the mind of both Cora and her brother. Who could it have been who tried to injure her in this way by throwing suspicion on her, and what could have been their motive?

She tried to reason certain things out. She went over in detail, while Walter was driving her car for her, every incident that she could remember in connection with the collision and the subsequent loss of the money.

She speculated on the actions of every one. Mary's desire to leave the car at the post-office and not go back to her shop was odd, Cora thought, though her employer had given Mary permission to go for a ride with such well-paying customers as the Kimballs and the Robinson twins. Next Cora tried to analyze Sid's actions, also those of Ida, and she even found herself wondering at Sid's seeming intimacy with Lem Gildy. But it all came to nothing. There was still that unanswered question: "Who took the money from the wallet?"

That the same person did so who had placed the empty pocketbook in the tool-box seemed evident.

Jack and Cora went together to tell Ed. Walter wanted to accompany them, but Cora insisted that she be allowed to tell the story first.

"Later Ed may want to question you," she declared.

The three members of the mandolin club were left at the Kimball home until Cora and Jack returned.

Ed at first was much startled by the news. Then he opened the wallet.

"They didn't leave anything," he said slowly.

"Is that all you want to remark?" asked Jack.

"All? Why, of course. What else can I say?"

"Well, don't you think—not to put too fine a point upon it—that it looks suspicious?"

"For whom?"

"Us—Cora," said Jack bluntly.

"Look here," began Ed fiercely; "if it wasn't you who said that—say—look here—- Oh, what nonsense! I hope, Cora, that you haven't for one moment thought that I would have the least suspicion against you."

"I—er—I—of course I didn't," she finished quickly. "Only Jack thought it looked queer."

"How foolish!" exclaimed Ed. "Why, it would be the easiest thing in the world for the thief to throw the empty pocketbook into your tool-box as the car was passing him in the street. The box isn't kept locked, is it?"

"No; not always."

"Then that's how it happened. The thief is around Chelton—that's evident. In order to divert suspicion he—"

"Or she," interrupted Jack with a smile.

"Yes, or she, if you like—he or she opened the box when your car was halted momentarily in the street, and dropped the wallet in. It's as simple as can be."

"But not so simple to find the thief," retorted Jack.

"Indeed not," agreed Ed with a rueful smile. "But I'll give the police this clue. It's a good one, I should think."

"And if they want to arrest me—why, I'll be at home," declared Cora with a laugh. "Would you like to see Walter?"

"No; you have told me all that is necessary."

Cora and Jack made a quick run back home, while Ed, went to communicate to the police the latest clue.

That evening, when Jack, Cora and the three college lads went down to the post-office, Cora happened to look in the window of the millinery shop where Mary Downs was employed. She was surprised to see on the big plate glass a sign: "Apprentice Wanted."

"That's odd," she mused. "I didn't suppose that Madam Julia could use two apprentices. I wonder if Mary has been discharged—for taking that ride with me. I must inquire."

The mail was late, and as the young people waited for it to be sorted they heard in the crowd talk indicating that the news of the finding of the empty wallet was known. Ed had told the police, and several reporters had also heard of the matter.

"Well, it's a very strange and romantic affair," remarked Angelina Bott, a sentimental sort of girl, to her chum, Alice Haven. "It would make quite a story."

"For the detectives—yes," assented Alice. Then, speaking so loudly that Cora could not help but hear, she added: "I guess hiders make the best finders, after all."

Cora's face turned red. Jack, with an angry retort on his lips, stepped forward, but his sister laid a detaining hand on his arm.

"Don't, Jack," she begged.

"But it's as good as saying you took it."

"I know; but—but, Jack, there will be more or less of—suspicion."

Jack swallowed a lump in his throat. He glared at Alice Haven, who looked coldly at him and then turned away.

Just then the windows were opened, indicating that the mail was sorted, and there was a rush on the part of the waiting crowd. Alice and Angelina were swallowed up in it.

Cora, with bitterness in her heart, turned aside. There were tears in her eyes, and she did not want Jack to see them.

As she looked down a corridor of the post-office, she saw a stooping figure hurrying along. It was that of Sid Wilcox. And from another corridor, crossing the main one, came a girl, who joined him.

The girl was Ida Giles, and as Cora watched them she saw Sid hand Ida something that showed white in the gleam of an incandescent lamp. It was evidently a letter.

CHAPTER XI

MOTORING OUTFITS

For days following the loss of the money and the finding of the empty pocketbook every possible clue was followed up, both by the police of New City and Chelton, and by many detectives, who were lured on by the offered reward of five hundred dollars.

Nor were suspicious tongues idle. If Cora was not openly accused, it was because she had a brother who would vigorously defend her. Nor did the Robinson girls altogether escape, though it was generally hinted, in the case of all the young ladies, that they might have hidden the money "just for fun," and when they saw what excitement it caused they were afraid to return it.

"As if that was a joke," said Cora, when she heard this version.

Of course, the boys who took part in the race had to answer numerous questions for the police, but at the end of a week, which was an unpleasant one for all concerned, the detectives were as far off the track as ever. Sid and Ida had their share of the "third degree" of police questioning in a mild form, and though Sid was at first indignant and refused to answer questions, he finally gave in. There was an unofficial verdict of "not guilty" in the case of all, and Ed's little fortune seemed likely never to be found.

When, about two weeks after the loss, Cora took a hundred-dollar bill to the bank to get it changed, and the teller looked at it rather longer than seemed necessary, Jack, who was with his sister, asked:

"What's the matter? Isn't that good?" He betrayed some feeling, for the finger of suspicion seemed pointing at his family from every person he met.

"Why—I hope it's good," was the smiling answer. "If it isn't I have lost faith in the government printing office."

"My grandmother gave it to me for my birthday," explained Cora. "I haven't had time to spend it since getting my auto. No one ever questioned a bill of hers before."

"Neither have I questioned it," declared the teller. "I was merely making a note of the number. We have instructions to take a memorandum of all bills of large denomination. I was merely doing that."

"Since when was that rule in effect?" asked Jack.

"Since the Foster robbery."

Jack started. Then he remembered that in Ed's wallet were bills of large denomination.

"Suspicion even here," he muttered to Cora as they went out.

"Hush, Jack, dear," she said softly. "Some folks will hear you."

"Well, I don't care if they do. It's fierce—the way people believe that you—and I—had a hand in that robbery."

"Never mind," replied his sister. "Oh," she added quickly, "there are the Robinson girls outside," and she hurried down the bank steps. The two sisters were walking slowly along, and from a certain air about Bess it was evident that she had something important to tell Cora.

"Any news of the—robbery?" Bess asked Jack.

"Not that I know of," he answered rather gloomily. "The trouble is that so many of those who might be able to throw additional light on it are away. Sid has gone—no one seems to know where—Ida is away visiting, and we haven't been able to find that old farmer that got his team in the way of the race. Ed remembers passing him on the road, and he spoke to him, but even that wouldn't account for how the wallet got in Cora's car."

"No," said Elizabeth with a sigh. "But where are you going, Cora?"

"Around to Madam Julia's. I went in the bank to get grandmother's hundred-dollar bill broken, so I could pay for my things at madam's. I suppose they are done by this time. Won't you girls come with me?"

"Yes," added Jack, "and speaking of hundred dollar bills, what do you suppose that bank teller did? He—"

"Jack, dear," spoke Cora softly, and her brother subsided.

"Do come," she urged the twins: "It will be such fun to see me try on my motor togs."

"Wait until we tell you something!" burst out Belle. "We have—"

"A surprise for you," interrupted Bess.

"A brand-new—" started in Belle.

"Motor car," finished Bess triumphantly.

"That is, we're going to get it," added her sister.

"Father has promised it to us;" supplemented Bess.

"Oh, isn't that splendid!" exclaimed Cora. "I'm so glad! This is a surprise. Now we'll all be motor girls."

"Yes," added Belle; "and mother said we could go this afternoon and select some motor things for ourselves at madam's. Isn't that just too sweet of her?"

"Lovely!" cried Cora, giving the twins a little hug in turn.

"Here, quit that in public. Want to make a fellow jealous?" demanded Jack.

"Oh—you—" began Belle with an arch look at Cora's brother.

"Now we're going to take a preliminary look at things with you, Cora," said Bess. "I'm just dying to get a certain bonnet that I saw in the window."

"Toot-toot! Farewell!" cried Jack, as he puffed in imitation of an auto and turned up the street.

"Do you know," began Cora as soon as her brother was safely out of sight, "speaking of that robbery, I have been thinking lately how strange it was that Ida, Mary and Sid should have been talking so seriously behind my car when I happened to look around and see them. Mary's face flushed, and Ida immediately walked away."

"Is that so?" demanded Bess.

"Yes, and I have been puzzling over it for some time."

"I overheard some of the things they said," declared Belle. "I think Sid was trying to get Mary and Ida to promise to go out for a ride with him that evening. Ida refused, and Mary—well, I didn't hear just what she said—but it wasn't no, I'm sure."

"But they all three looked so—so guilty," went on Cora. "It was exactly as if they didn't want to be discovered."

"Maybe Sid was ashamed to be seen asking Mary to go for a ride. You know, he's reported to be well off, and Mary—well, she's a dear, sweet little girl, but she works for a living, and you know what a fellow like Sid thinks of working girls."

"I thought I heard Sid saying something about hiring a machine to take them out in," went on Belle.

"Well, maybe we'll get a chance to ask Mary about it when we get to madam's," said Cora. "She'll be sent in to help us try on our things."

They were soon in front of the shop with the big' glass front—the only real, big glass front in Chelton—and behind the plate was displayed a single hat—a creation—as Madam Julia described it. Madam Julia was very exclusive.

The door-boy, a dapper little colored chap, in an exceedingly tight-fitting suit of blue, with innumerable brass buttons on it, in double rows in front, in triple rows behind, and in single rows on sleeves, opened the portal for the young ladies, bowing low as he did so.

"I guess this is Mary coming now," said Cora in a low voice as she heard some one approaching from behind the silken draperies that separated part of the shop.

But the three customers looked up in surprise when a strange young girl appeared through the parted curtains.

"Miss Kimball," said Cora, announcing her own name, for she had an appointment.

"Oh, yes," was the girl's answer. "I will tell madam."

"Where is Mary?" whispered Bess.

"That accounts for the sign I saw," spoke Cora, telling her chums of the notice that an apprentice was wanted. "Mary must have been discharged. Madam would never keep two—in Chelton."

Madam Julia, as she was always called, entered with a swish of skirts and leaving a trail of French instructions behind her in the work-room—instructions to her employees as to the trimming on this "effect" and the reshaping of that "creation."

"Ah, yes, Mees Kimball," she began. "I am all in readiness —but—pardon—zat Marie—she haf left me—in such hastiness—I am all at what you call ze ocean—how you express it?"

With a pretty little motion of her hands she looked appealingly at Cora.

"You mean all at sea, madam."

"Ah, yes! At sea! How comprehensive! Ze sea is always troubled, and so am I. Zat Marie she left me so suddenness—I know not where are all my things—I depend so much on her—"

"Has Miss Downs left?" Cora could not refrain from asking.

"Ha! Yes! Zat is eet. Precisely. So quickly she go away an' leaf me. She does not think much about it, perhaps, but I am too busy to be so annoyed. Just some relation not well—indisposition, maybe—well—voila! she is gone—it was not so in my time that a girl must leaf her trade and depart with such quickness—run away. Louise! Louse! Come instantly and for me find zat motor chapeau for Mademoiselle Kimball."

Her voice rose to a shrill call.

"Quick!" she called, and then came a string of French. "I must not be kept waiting—eet was already packed—"

Louise, who had replaced Mary Downs, found the bonnet Cora had ordered, and handed it to her mistress. Cora took her place before a mirror, and madam began patting the motor cap hood affectionately over the girl's black tresses.

"It will suit you to perfection!" exclaimed the French woman. "You have ze hair beautiful. Zere!" She brushed the hood down over Cora's ears. "Zat is ze way. Do not wear a motor hood as if it was a tiara! Zat is of a hatefulness! Such bad taste! Voila—what is it zat you Americans say?—ze fitness of zings. Yes, zat is what I mean."

The hood certainly looked well on Cora. Bess and Belle nodded their approval. It was of the old-fashioned Shaker type, of delicate pongee silk, and showed off to advantage Cora's black, wavy fair, as it fell softly about her temples.

"Es eet not becoming?" demanded madam, and then she became profuse in her native tongue. "Zat—what you call Shaker—eet is ze prettiest—so chic—voila!" and once more she patted it on Cora's head.

Cora was very well pleased with it. Then the mask was brought out. This was a simple affair—Cora only wanted such things as were practical. The mask, which had been specially designed to suit the girl, was nothing more than a piece of veiling, with the goggles set in. The veil was secured to the hood by a simple shirr string of elastic.

Madam slipped it over Cora's face.

"Zere!" the milliner exclaimed.

"Lovely!" declared Bess.

"Very beautiful!" added Belle.

Louise, the little girl helper, gave a wonder look of admiration. Louise had well-trained eyes.

"Would you know me?" asked Cora with a little laugh.

"Never!" replied Bess. "Won't it be splendid? Suppose we all get things alike? Then we can travel—incog!"

"Oh, jolly!" cried Belle. "Just fancy Walter asking me to have soda, and he thinking I'm some one else!"

Cora laughed merrily at Belle's joke. Walter's preference for Cora was no secret.

"How about my cloak?" asked Cora.

"Not quite ready," replied madam. "You see, zat naughty Marie, leaving me so—"

"Did you say some of her relatives were ill?" ventured Bess.

"I believe so. Some aunt, away in some far place. Marie is gone to her."

Louise took the mask and hood from Cora and flitted away with them beyond the silk curtains. There was to be a stitch taken here, and a little, tacking up was needed there. The veil was to be a bit closer, the milliner explained.

Next Madam Julia turned to the twins.

"My friends wish to see about some motor things, also," remarked Cora. "What would you think of having them all alike—for us there?"

This brought on such a discussion, madam talking more in French than English, and Belle was kept busy translating for her sister.

The madam preferred giving the young ladies such hoods and cloaks as would best suit their complexions. Bess should have a brown one—just running to the shade of her hair, but not quite reaching it, and Belle needed a dark blue—for only a true blond can wear dark blue and not look old in it.

So madam explained. But the twins would not decide, after all, until their mother could be consulted, so the order was not definitely placed.

When they were about to leave, and madam had vanished behind the silken draperies, Bess turned to one of the hat sticks, upon which rested a most conspicuous piece of headgear.

"Oh, look at that!" she exclaimed. "Isn't it awful?"

"It certainly is ridiculous!" chimed in Belle, taking the motor hood, for such it was, off the support and holding it up for inspection.

"That's certainly what madam calls a 'creation,'" said Cora.

"Who in the world would ever wear that?" asked Bess with a laugh.

"I expected to," unexpectedly replied a voice behind them. The three girls turned quickly to confront Ida Giles. She had come in so quietly that they had not heard her. Cora, Belle and Bess looked dumfounded.

"And perhaps in the future," went on Ida in icy tones, "it would be just as well to leave another person's hat alone."

"I beg your pardon," Cora managed to say, "We—er—we were just—interested in motor hoods."

"And making fun of mine!" snapped Ida.

Louise had entered to attend to the new customer. Ida turned to her:

"I wish to see Madam Julia!" she exclaimed. Outside Bess burst into her full, hearty laugh.

Then the three motor girls made their escape.

"I thought I would choke in there!" she exclaimed.

"Lucky for you that Ida didn't take a hand in, helping you out in the choking process," remarked Cora. "She looked as if she would like to have done it."

"But what in the world do you suppose she wants with a motor hood?" asked Belle.

"To ride with Sid, of course," answered Cora.

"But his machine is out of order, and he as much as said that he didn't intend to get it fixed right away," persisted Belle.

"Maybe he's going to get a new one," ventured Cora.

"I don't see how he can," replied Belie. "I heard father say he was dreadfully in debt. His folks had some dealings with father, I believe, about advancing him some money that is to come to him when he is a certain age, but it won't be for some time yet. They had to have some to pay his debts."

"You ought not to repeat that, Belle," cautioned Bess. "You know father would be displeased if he knew you had spoken of his private affairs."

"Well, I'm sure it will go no further—with Cora," retorted Belle. "I wouldn't mention it to any one else."

"Of course, I'll not repeat it," promised Cora. "But what do you think .about Mary leaving so suddenly?"

"I don't know what to think," replied Bess. "It looks odd. to say the least. What reason would she have for leaving town so-well, mysteriously, to put it mildly?"

"Of course, it may be a mere coincidence," went on Cora, "but in connection with her talk with Ida and Sid—well, I have often noticed that matters conspire to 'look strange' whenever there is a chance of making complications."

CHAPTER XII

A RACE AGAINST TIME

It was a few days after the visit to Madam Julia that Cora was out alone in the Whirlwind. She had been feeling very unhappy over the loss of Ed's money and the suspicion that naturally attached to her on account of the finding of the empty wallet in her car. She could not dismiss the matter from her mind.

But Ed Foster had done everything in his power to make her feel that she was in no wise concerned. He had called and taken dinner with Jack, and had announced that, as far as he could see, he feared he would have to charge the money and bonds up to profit and loss.

"Principally loss," he remarked with a rueful smile. "I don't believe those detectives will ever get it."

Jack had offered to go with his sister when she announced that she was about to take a run in her car, but, with a little nod of thanks, she declined his company.

"It's a beautiful morning," she said, "and I want to take a good, long ride by myself, Jack. I want to—think. I feel that the air will do me more good than anything else."

Her mother had gone into town, and once his offer was refused, Jack took a book and declared that he was going to try to work off some of his college conditions. The Robinson girls were at their music lessons, Cora knew, so he would not call for them. Thus she started off alone.

Down the turnpike she steered the big machine, confident in her ability to manage it. There were few autos out, and the highway was almost deserted. Her pretty Shaker hood, which had lately come home from Madam Julia's, was unbound, and the loose, chiffon strings flew out in the wind like long-legged birds. Turning into a broad avenue, Cora realized that she was on the road leading to the garage where she had met Paul Hastings, the handsome chauffeur who had given her such valuable information about her car.

"I must see about getting the mud guard fixed," she reflected, for the temporary brace that Ed had made, though it had kept the affair in place until the day previous had now come loose. "And this is a good time to have it attended to," thought the girl.

Paul Hastings was in the little front office. He smiled pleasantly at the flushed girl as she told her needs, but somehow he seemed dejected—as if something had happened. Even Cora, comparative stranger that she was to him, could not help inquiring the cause of his trouble.

"Is—is there anything the matter?" she asked hesitatingly.

"Oh—not much. Only I—er—I have just ex experienced quite a loss, and it makes me—blue."

"That's too bad!"

"Yes," he went on. "I had an opportunity of getting a first-class position, but another fellow got ahead of me."

"How's that?"

'Well, you see, a firm in New City needs a manager. I have good backing, and was almost certain of the place. But another fellow had just as good a chance, and it was a question of who got there first. I was delayed here and missed the only train that would bring me there on time. He caught it, and is now on his way there. He'll get the place and I—won't."

"But why don't you take a machine and go there? You can do it as quickly as the train can."

"Take a machine?" he repeated. "I wouldn't dare. I'd be sure to lose my place here, and might not get the other. I haven't a car in the place I would dare risk taking out on the road. The owners are too particular about them, and I can't blame them, either."

Cora thought for a moment. A daring plan came into her mind.

"Let me take you," she suggested.

"Oh, indeed, I would not think of such a thing. I should not have mentioned my troubles to you. But they were so—so much to me that I didn't realize what I was doing. But let me look at your car."

He soon adjusted the broken bolt of the mud guard, and announced that it was now as good as new.

"But why won't you go in the Whirlwind?" demanded the girl. "I am only out on a little pleasure spin, and I would be very glad indeed to take you to New City. Besides, I'd like to race with the train," she went on with sparkling eyes. "I know I could beat it."

Paul looked interested.

"I guess you could," he said. "It would be a good chance, anyhow."

"Come on, then! Don't waste a moment. Let's try it."

Paul called his assistant, a young lad, and gave him instructions about some cars, and what to do if certain customers came in. It was not a busy part of the day, and he could leave without causing any complications. Then he slipped into his long, linen coat and stepped into Cora's car.

"I'm afraid this is an imposition," he declared, taking the steering wheel, a sort of unconscious habit he had. Then he bethought himself. "Oh, but I suppose you'll drive," he added quickly, shifting over, rather abashed at having taken his place in the driver's seat without being asked. "You see, I'm so accustomed to being here."

"I believe I will drive," answered Cora. "I have great faith in the obedience of my machine. It knows my hand."

"I shouldn't wonder," agreed the young, man. "I do believe that motor-cars can almost be made to think—under the guidance of very gentle but sure hands."

Paul looked very handsome, Cora thought. He was the type she always admired—a youth with a bronze complexion—a straight, athletic figure, almost classic, Cora decided. He cranked up for her, re-entered the car, and they rolled from the garage. Once out on the country road Cora threw in the high gear and fed the gasolene with a judicious hand, controlling the spark admirably.

"A fine machine!" exclaimed Paul, noting how perfect was the rhythm of action as it thrilled out beneath them.

"There are friends of mine," said Cora suddenly as a runabout, containing two young then, came into sight. Ed Foster and Walter Pennington raised their caps as they dashed by, but they did not go so quickly but that Cora noticed an expression of surprise on their faces.

"Oh, yes, I know them also," remarked Paul. "I've had that machine in the garage."

"I wonder where they are going?" went on Cora. She also found herself wondering if Walter and Ed were surprised to see her out alone with a professional chauffeur. It was the first time her conduct in taking Paul with her came forcibly to her mind. Then, with an independence of spirit that characterized her, she decided she had no apology or explanation to make.

"It's hard to say where any person in an auto is going," replied Paul pleasantly, "and sometimes almost as hard to say when they'll get there."

"That young man on the right is the one who recently lost twenty thousand dollars," observed the girl as she changed to second speed to take a troublesome little hill.

"So I understand. And wasn't there some mystery connected with it?"

"Indeed, there was. You know, they found the empty wallet in the tool-box of my car."

"Yes, so I heard. Quite remarkable. But can't the detectives find out who stole the money and hid the pocketbook there?"

Cora was grateful for the neat way he put that, to avoid referring to the suspicions that had been cast on her and on her friends.

"The police don't appear able to do anything," was her answer. "It does seem very strange."

"Have they inquired of all the people who were on hand at the time of the robbery—or loss—when, I understand, it was very likely that the empty wallet was put in your tool-box?"

"Oh, yes, they have questioned all of us—and I can tell you that they were not any too polite about it, either. I thought I would never get over their quizzing."

"Well, I suppose they have to be sharp," remarked Paul. "But I've not yet explained to you the reason why I am in such a hurry and the nature of the position I am after. You see, a firm in New City advertised for a chauffeur to drive their machine across the country in a big race. I replied, and was as good as engaged. I expected to go over this morning, but some one told me that Sid Wilcox had taken the early train and was going to beat me out—It's a case of first come—get the job, you see."

"Sidney Wilcox!" exclaimed Cora in astonishment.

"Yes. You know him, of course. It seems that he wants to make the trip, and is willing to run the machine without pay. I can't afford to do that, and that gives him an advantage over me. If Sid gets there first, and offers to do it for nothing, it means that they'll take him."

"Well, he'll not get there first!" exclaimed Cora very determinedly.

Suddenly they both heard the distant whistle of the train. "There she is!" cried Paul; and a little later they caught sight of the cars, flying over the track.

"We're too late," said Paul.

"Not yet," answered Cora. "We can take a shorter route, even if they can go faster than we can."

She was already running on third speed, and the motor was taking about all the gasolene it could use. She adjusted the spark to give the best service, and now, as an additional means of inducing speed, she cut out the muffler. The explosions of the motor played a tattoo on the dusty road.

"I'm going to turn here!" cried Cora as she swung around a corner. "Look out!"

Paul needed no warning, for he was an expert autoist. The machine skidded a bit and tilted somewhat, but was soon flying down the straight, level stretch.

"I cannot understand why Sid Wilcox wants to run in a cross-country race—and for nothing," said Cora.

"Because he knows I want the place. He hates me and wants to make trouble for me."

"Is that so? Then we have a double reason for beating him. And I think we'll do it. His train has to wait for the accommodation to pass it at the junction. We'll gain on him there."

"That's so."

"What time is it now?" Cora asked as, with hands firmly gripping the wheel, she leaned forward to peer down the road. She could neither see nor hear the train now.

"It's nine-fifty-five," replied the chauffeur. "The train is due at New City at ten-fifteen."

"Twenty minutes yet. I'm sure we can make it."

Cora made that declaration with her cheeks flushing and her bright eyes ablaze with excitement.

"Won't you, let me take the wheel?" asked Paul. "I am afraid that this heavy driving is too much for you."

"Oh, no, indeed! This is my race, you know. I want to beat him."

She looked at Paul frankly.

"Very well. Only don't distress yourself too much—on my account."

"Don't worry. I love this. At what place in New City do you wish to go?"

"Directly in the center, next to the bank. The office of the Whitehall Motor Company."

"Then we'll take this road," decided the girl. "I'm sure it cuts through a park, and will bring us out right at the center of the city."

"It does, and it's the nearest way. You're getting to be quite a driver."

"I mean to be. Hark, there's the train again!"

"Yes, and we're ahead of it!" exclaimed Paul as he caught sight of the cars. "We've gained on them!"

"But they're going down grade, and we have a hill to climb," spoke Cora a little despairingly. But she would not give up. On and on rushed the car. There was but five minutes left, and the railroad; station was very close to the building where the automobile concern was located. Sid's chances were very good—Paul's not quite so much so.

"We'll have to be a little careful now," Paul reminded her as they swung around a curve. "We'll have to go slow through the city."

"Yes, but I have been counting on that. We still have a few minutes. Oh, isn't it a pity that a motor isn't like a horse? When you get a machine going just so fast it can't go any faster, but a horse can always be depended on for a spurt."

"Yes," answered Paul quietly. He was busy thinking.

"How many minutes lift now?" asked Cora.

"Two," was the grim answer.

With keen eyes, that took note of every obstruction or vehicle that might block her, Cora drove her car on. Around corners, and through busy streets she piloted it. They were but a block from the center of the town.

"There's the train," spoke Paul quietly as the engine pulled into the station.

"And we're at the building of the Whitehall auto concern!" exclaimed Cora triumphantly a few seconds later, as she guided the car up to the curb. "Hurry!" she called to Paul. As if he needed to be told that!

He leaped from the car and ran across the pavement to the office. As he entered the door Sid Wilcox, coming leisurely from the direction of the station, saw him. Sid started, and then, with a quick motion, hurried after Paul. But the chauffeur was ahead of him, and the door slammed shut in the face of the owner of the Streak.

Paul, thanks to Cora's aid, had won the race against time.

"Oh, I do hope he gets the place," she said as she stopped her engine and prepared to rest while Paul was within the office of the motor company.

CHAPTER XIII

THE STOLEN RIDE

Cora was of a very independent character. She felt that she had done right, and she did not care who knew it. But, for all that, she could not help whispering to herself:

"I'm glad Sid didn't see me bringing Paul here. He evidently thought he had plenty of time. He didn't look my way, and, besides, I had my veil down." Sid had disappeared after Paul.

She decided that she would not wait in the main street for Paul, as he might be kept some time, but would spin through the park. She was about to start when Sid Wilcox reappeared. His face showed his anger, but at the sight of Cora in her car he called up a smile to his countenance.

"Why, good-morning," he said pleasantly, stepping up to the auto. "You look as though you had been speeding," for her face was flushed from the wind.

"A little," was her smiling response. She could afford to smile now.

"Waiting for some one?" he asked.

"Yes."

It was too late to start off now:

"I'm waiting, too. Suppose I get in and take a turn around the park with you? You've never invited me to try your new car."

Cora was surprised. She knew very well she had not asked him to ride in the Whirlwind, and she had no intention of doing so. She was about to reply, when Sid jumped in beside her.

"I see you're not going to ask me," he went on, "and, as I have no idea of losing the chance for a spin, I'll get in without an invitation."

With a quick motion he shoved over the spark lever and the motor started, for a charge had remained in one of the cylinders, obviating the necessity of cranking up.

"There, we're all ready to go," he said.

Cora was dumfounded. But she felt it would not do to make a vigorous protest in such a public place. For a moment her feelings threatened to master her. Then she regained control of herself, threw in the clutch and turned the car in the direction of the park. After all, it might be better to humor Sid.

"So you brought Paul Hastings over?" drawled the youth.

Then he had seen her, after all. Cora's precautions were useless.

She nodded coldly. She was offended by her companion's impertinent tone. She started to turn off the power and apply the brake. She would not ride with him.

"Oh, you needn't get mad," continued Sid quickly. "I did not mean to offend you, though if it had not been for you Paul would not have gotten here ahead of me. You're a plucky girl, as well as a pretty one."

Cora flashed an indignant look at him.

"I suppose you meant that for a compliment," she said, "but you don't quite understand the art. It requires a certain delicacy—"

"Such as Paul Hastings might have," sneered Sid.

Cora felt that she could not bear with him a moment longer.

"I have a purchase to make here," she said with as much frigidness in her tones as she could call up. "I'll not ask you to wait," and she stopped the car in front of a dress-goods store.

"Oh, it's no trouble to wait."

"I'd rather you wouldn't."

"Well, I will." He was smiling now. "I never like to leave a young lady when she is in a—temper."

Cora was positively angry. But again came that detestation of making a scene, which every well-bred girl feels, no matter how strong the provocation. She would make a purchase to gain time, and then turn back to the bank building.

She bought something she was in no need of, and prolonged the transaction to an interminable length, to the no small disgust of the salesgirl. When she got back to the machine, Sid was smiling more broadly than before.

He had taken her place at the wheel.

"You won't mind me driving as far as the bank building, will you?" he said. "I really must get a new car. I miss mine so much, and it's in bad shape since you—-er—tried to smash me."

"I did nothing of the sort. It was your own fault."

"There, there," he said soothingly. "We mustn't quarrel."

Cora felt herself growing pale. She repressed a stinging reply, and without a word took a seat in the tonneau.

"Oh, so you won't sit beside me?" he asked as he started the car. "What makes you dislike me so, Cora? You and I used to pull a pretty good stroke, but lately you simply won't look at me."

"I don't dislike you. At least, I did not until this morning."

"Still angry," he taunted. "Now, I call that mean. Why do you go off riding with a common mechanic?"

"Mr. Hastings is a gentleman!" she flared back at him, like an explosion of one of the cylinders of her car. "He would never dream of acting as you are now, even if he is a common mechanic."

"No?"

His tone was tantalizing.

"Please turn this corner," she said icily. "I want to get back to the bank building."

"Oh, do you? Well, I'm in no hurry to. I can't seem to do any business there, or in the automobile place," and he flashed a meaning look at the girl. "Now we'll see, Miss Cora, who's going to have their own way. I'm driving this car."

He threw in the second speed gear, and the auto dashed forward through the city streets.

Had he suddenly gone mad? What was his object? He was heading for the turnpike road!

For a few moments Cora held her breath. Should she shout for help, no matter what happened?

Then the fact of her unfortunate entanglement with the missing money came to her mind.

Should she deliberately place herself in the position of another entanglement?

Sid Wilcox bent lower over the steering wheel and turned on more power.

"Paul Hastings rode out with you," he called over his shoulder to Cora, "and I'm going to ride back with you. Nothing like having a variety and being a popular young lady."

He was positively insulting.

"You are running away with my car!" exclaimed Cora, stung to desperation. "I shall have you arrested!"

"Oh, no, you won't!" he sneered. "That would not be at all pleasant—for you!"

"Why do you say that?"

"Why? Because you might have to explain how that pocketbook got into your car. I heard last night that they were going to have another investigation on new lines."

"How dare you!" she cried. "But that has nothing to do with this. If you do not stop my car at once I shall call for help!"

"I dare you to!"

Did he know that she would not?

"Now, Cora, Cora," he simpered. "You must not do anything rash. Better let me have my little ride with you, and incidentally get ahead of my conceited rival, Paul Hastings. He may ride back in the car he is to drive across country, for he has probably done me out of that place. It will be a good chance for him to practice."

Sid's audacity was positively startling. Perhaps it would be best to let him have his own way. In fact, how could she help herself? He had the wheel, and was going at a fast rate of speed. She could not climb over to a front seat from the tonneau. If she should shout, who would hear her above the noise of the car? For Sid in mere spitefulness had cut out the muffler.

Cora sank back in utter disgust and despair. What ever would Paul Hastings think of her? What would Walter Pennington say? Whoever saw her, it would make talk. Besides, Paul had come to New City in his shop clothes concealed under his duster, a fitting enough suit in which to ride in an auto, but not if he had to go back in the train. Perhaps, she thought, he had not brought money enough with him, depending on her to take him back to Chelton.

And, above all, what would people think of Cora Kimball riding with Sidney Wilcox?

"This is glorious!" exulted the daring youth, "I have just been pining for a ride in this car, Cora, and, incidentally, I may as well admit that I have been pining for a talk with you. When have you heard from your friend, Miss Downs?"

He fairly shot the question at Cora.

"Miss Downs?" she said falteringly.

"Yes."

"I don't know that I ever hear from Mary Downs," was Cora's sharp reply,

"No?" His voice was queerly questioning. "Well, I want to say I think Mary a very slick little girl."

Cora could not mistake his intention. He wanted her to think that he believed Mary was not one of her set. By "slick" he probably meant to convey the idea that he considered the former milliner girl might be tricky.

"I am sorry Miss Downs is away," said Cora simply. "I intended to take her on a little run with me. She doesn't get many chances to go out in a car."

"No, I guess, not. But don't you think it—er—rather risky to take up with—shop girls?"

"Shop girls? Why, any girl is a lady, no matter what her position, as long as she conducts herself like one. What do you mean by your insinuations?"

She almost detested herself for asking him this question, but she could not help it.

Sid laughed.

"What have you to say against her character?" demanded Cora again.

Sid seemed a bit uneasy. He had hardly expected to be pinned down so directly.

"Oh, of course," he finally answered, "if you feel that way about it, I—er—I suppose—nothing. I only wished to caution you. That money matter is still in—er—well, let us say, in an awkward shape."

"Does Mary Downs know anything about it?" asked Cora directly, determined to face Sid down.

"I'm sure I don't know," he drawled. "But you know she was —er—there with the—rest of us."

CHAPTER XIV

JUST CORA AND PAUL

As if this had been the entire object of his peculiar actions, Sid suddenly stopped the car.

"This is as far as I care to go," he said. "I think I'll leave you now. I can't thank you enough for the ride," he added mockingly, and, with a bow that had much of irony in it, he walked down a side path of the park, into which he had directed the machine.

Cora did not answer him, but her look was sufficient to show what she thought. And in spite of her contempt she felt an overwhelming desire to question him about what he had said of Mary Downs.

Did Sid Wilcox know anything about the robbery?

That was a question Cora asked herself as she took her place at the wheel, just vacated by the unmannerly youth.

"He certainly acts as though he did," she reasoned to herself. "And why should he make such an insinuation against Mary?"

She found no answer to her question. Suddenly looking at her watch she noted that no train had departed from New City since she and Paul had reached there. She was yet in time to give, him a ride home as she had planned. Turning quickly she made the run back toward the bank building.

From behind a clump of bushes Sid Wilcox watched her.

"I wonder if you'll tell your brother?" he mused, "If you do there may be a row over my kidnaping you. But I couldn't help it. No, I don't think you will tell Jack. You don't want to see us—quarrel."

He added the last word below his breath, and there was a mean smile on his face. As he turned to continue his walk he met a man coming in the opposite direction.

"Lem Gildy! What are you doing here?" he exclaimed.

"Why—er—I'm sort of lookin' for work."

"You—work!" exclaimed Sid.

"Well, I heard you was goin' to take a trip across country, and I thought maybe you'd take me along. You and me's pals, ain't we?"

"Hush!" exclaimed Sid, as if afraid of someone hearing the man's words. "Don't you know better than to follow me?"

"Well, I heard you was comin' for a new job, an' I thought—"

"You think entirely too much. Now you get hack to Chelton, and stay there. I may need you."

Lem's little, rat-like eyes gleamed.

"You'll pay me, won't you?" he asked.

"Of course."

"Well, I'm a little short now, an'—"

Sid extended a bill, which the man took quickly.

"Now be off," ordered young Wilcox, "and don't ever follow me again."

He waited until Lem had shuffled off, and then he took a different path.

"He's getting altogether too familiar," said Sid to himself as he strolled along. "But I may find him useful."

Scarcely had Cora, driving her big car, turned into the turnpike leading from the park to New City, than she again encountered Ed Foster and Walter Pennington. She instantly realized that they would wonder why she did not stop, for Ed was slowing up his car. But she knew she could not get back to the bank building to meet Paul if she halted, so, with a smile, as comprehensive as she was able to make it, she sent the Whirlwind ahead at a fast speed. She noted the looks of surprise on the faces of her friends as she passed them.

"How ever will I be able to explain?" was the thought that flashed into Cora's mind. "Walter acted as if he wanted to say something— perhaps something about the money. He looked as if he were pleased. Maybe he has some good news."

It took Cora but a short time to make the run back to the city. She turned her machine toward the depot, as she knew a train would shortly leave for Chelton, and she fancied Paul might try to get it. Reaching the station she saw his tall figure, clad in the linen duster, pacing up and down the platform. She was just in time.

"Did you think I ran away?" she asked as she skillfully turned the car up to the platform and stopped.

"Oh, no," he replied with a happy laugh. "I happened to see who got into the car, and I guessed that you were run away with."

"Wasn't it contemptible of him?" she asked, her fate flushing at the recollection of the ride. "But perhaps some day I may be able to make him realize it. He doesn't seem to—now."

"No; he isn't that kind."

"I was afraid I wouldn't be in time to take you back, after your interview with the automobile people, and I fancied you had not come prepared for a train trip to Chelton."

"That's very kind of you. I'm sorry you took the trouble to return. You have put yourself out considerably on my account, I'm afraid."

"Indeed, I have not. I enjoyed it myself—the ride, I mean —er—that is, the first ride," and she laughed nervously. "I'm glad we beat Sid. I fancy he acted as he did for revenge. But were you successful?"

"Very much so, thanks to you."

"Well, if you want to ride back with me, I'll be very glad to have you. I must get back in time for luncheon or mamma may worry."

"Well, we mustn't have that happen. I'll get right in," which he did, after cranking up the car for her, for not always could she stop it leaving a charge in one cylinder, so that it would start from the seat.

"I'm very glad you got the place," went on Cora as she steered out from among a tangle of other autos and carriages about the station.

"So am I. It means a great deal to me."

"And Sid was so disappointed. I could tell by his face, though he pretended not to be. But that's why he—ran away with me—or, rather, with my car."

"It would be difficult to understand all his reasons," declared Paul with a smile. "He may have had another, equally weighty."

"You mean—"

Cora felt the warm blood mounting to her cheeks.

"I think he wanted to boast that he had ridden with you."

Paul was rather sorry he had said this, the moment after the words were uttered. Cora seemed much embarrassed. To give a new direction to her thoughts, Paul said:

"I want to tell you about my sister. It was on her account that I particularly wished to get this position. Hazel wants to go to college, and we couldn't afford to send her. Now, with the increase in salary which I shall get, it will be possible."

"Oh, how nice!" exclaimed Cora. "What college is she going to?"

"I don't know yet. But she is very ambitious."

"I should judge that—from knowing her brother."

"That's very nice of you," he said, and then both laughed.

"I'd like to meet your sister," Cora remarked; without thinking of all her words might imply.

"Would you?" he asked warmly. "I'll be glad to have you. I think she's a mighty fine girl."

"Won't you hate to leave her when you make the run across country?"

"Well, it isn't to start for a month, but I shall have to go to New City to get familiar with the new machine I am to drive. I'm not going away at once. I'll be in New City for some time."

"Oh," began Cora, "I'm glad—"

She stopped, and again felt herself blushing. Her tone had been a little too warm. She realized that her evident pleasure and polite interest might be misinterpreted. It looked very much as if Cora was glad that Paul was not going away at once.

"Then your sister will not be deprived of your company just yet," she managed to say, and she seemed to be paying particular attention to the sparking lever.

"No," he replied. "Hazel and I are great friends—chums, you might say. In fact, I've never had a boy friend with whom I was able to get along so well as I can with my sister."

"That's very nice. It's what Jack says about me. He and I are the best of friends. Of course, I'm very fond of the Robinson girls, but Jack comes first. You remember the pretty twins, I've no doubt?"

"Yes, indeed I do. I could not help thinking how very 'untwinly' they are for twins."

"Aren't they? But they are the dearest girls! And they are going to have a new car."

"Is that so? Do you happen to know what kind?"

Paul assumed his professional air.

"I believe it has not been decided yet. But they will most likely get it from the Whitehall Company. Would you like to turn in the order?"

"It would be quite a help for me to be able to sell a car now, so soon after taking a place with them. And the commission—just as I am starting—"

"I think I can manage it easily enough," she said quickly. "They are sure to consult Jack about it. Couldn't you come over to our house this evening, and—"

Again she found herself stopping suddenly and blushing. It was rather awkward to ask a young man to call, particularly when one has never been properly introduced to him. If he were only acquainted with Jack, now . . .

Then Cora had a bright thought.

"You say you are acquainted with Walter Pennington?" she asked.

"Oh, yes. Our folks and the Penningtons are old friends."

"Then we must fix up a plan—er—to be perfectly proper. Not that it makes any difference. First I want to meet your sister. After that I am going to give a small affair. I have been putting it off for some time—it's a positive duty, but I've been so interested in my machine. There—I have it! I think I'll give an auto affair."

"Great possibilities in it," observed Paul. "But please do not trouble yourself to get up one on account of myself or my sister, though I appreciate—"

"Oh, no, indeed," Cora hastened to explain. "I am due to give one, anyhow, and it may as well be that. I will be doubly interested if there should happen to be a matter of business for you involved in it. The twins are in no great hurry about their car. When you can meet them properly, and I will arrange it, I am sure they will give you the order."

"That would be splendid. I can't thank you enough."

"Wait until you get the order," and she laughed, "Mother declares I have a positive faculty for business."

"I rather agree with her," said Paul with a smile, as his fair companion turned the machine into the main street of Chelton. "I really feel unable to properly thank you for what you have done for me to-day—"

"Now, please," interrupted Cora. "I was amply repaid in beating Sid Wilcox. But I cannot understand why he wanted the position. Even your explanation will hardly account for his extraordinary conduct. Why should he want to run a car across country?"

"Well, it can't be because he is short of funds," said Paul frankly. "I'm positive of that. He took particular pains to display a roll of bills when he was in the auto office, and I think that did not favorably impress the manager, though I was practically sure of the place when he came in."

"Well, that's just like Sid Wilcox," and Cora shuddered. It was a reaction of the unpleasant ride she had been forced to take with him.

"I hope, Miss Kimball, that you will soon be able to meet my sister," said Paul after a little silence, during which the car had run along. They were near the Beachwood Road, at the end of which, in a little grove of trees, was Cora's home.

"Not on account of what you have done for me," he went on, "but because I am sure you and she would be good friends. Hazel is a fine girl, as I said before, and besides that—" Paul stopped abruptly.

"Oh, I'm going to meet Hazel," declared Cora warmly as Paul alighted from the car. "I'll invite her to my affair. I am going to wake up folks around here. Do you know, we all seem to be terribly depressed since that money was—lost."

"Yes, and I don't wonder at it. Twenty thousand dollars is a large sum. I'd call it a fortune. But, somehow, I feel sure that Mr. Foster will recover it. I wish I could help unravel the mystery. I would like to—for more reasons than one."

What could he mean by that? His manner was very earnest. Cora glanced at him gratefully.

"Good-by," she said suddenly.

"Good-by," echoed Paul, and he turned up the street.

CHAPTER XV

THREE GIRLS

Reflecting on her strange experience while in New City, seated late that same afternoon on the broad veranda of her handsome home, Cora had one gratifying thought. No one whom she knew had seen her while Sid Wilcox was in possession of her car—and of her.

Feeling this assurance she decided not to mention to any one at home the fact of his having stolen the ride. She resolved to ask Paul to keep it a secret, and she knew he would. As for Sid himself, if he did boast of it, few would credit his story, for he did not bear a very good reputation for truth, and he was constantly getting into scrapes. Cora especially hoped Jack would not hear of the escapade.

Now Cora, who had been sitting in an easy chair, trying to read a book, decided to take the hammock for a change. She did not feel like reading.

She wore a simple frock of white muslin, and her hair was let down in a most becoming fashion, in long, loose braids, all combining to make her particularly girlish-looking.

Cora was taking what she called her "loll." This particular form of rest, she always declared, was the only sort a healthy girl could reasonably enjoy.

"When you rest, why, just rest," she used to say to Isabel Robinson, who, on account of her nervous temperament, had rather been overdone with "rest cure" ideas. Isabel delighted in such terms as "relaxation" and "siesta," while Cora reveled in her "loll."

A box of "deadly chocolates"—that is what Isabel would have called them—were at Cora's elbow, and she was just reaching for the tenth one, when Isabel herself, and her sister, sauntered along the path.

"Come on up, girls," called out Cora. "But please don't ask me to move. I'm in the most delicious heap."

"Exactly that!" exclaimed Isabel, who looked particularly pretty in a soft-blue summer gown, while Elizabeth was like some flower, in deep-pink muslin. "You do get into the most awful heaps, Cora, dear. But you never can rest without relaxing, and to do that—"

"Belle!" exclaimed Cora, "that is precisely why you never rest—you never relax your brain. You're always thinking of resting and not doing it."

Bess sank into a wicker chair and smothered the cushions. Bess was stout—"when she sat down," as Cora expressed it.

"Got your car ordered yet?" asked the hostess, passing around the box of chocolates. Neither girl could resist them.

"Oh, no," answered Belle. "Poor papa is in the greatest muddle. Every one in New City seems to have the best car to sell, and, as he wants a good one, he doesn't know which one to select."

"Why not ask Jack?" suggested Cora. "He's had lots of experience."

"Just what I proposed," replied Belle. "You, know how queer poor, dear papa is. He really dislikes motors."

"Seen Ida lately?" asked Bess.

"Not a sight of her," answered Cora. "I was hoping you might bring some news—not particularly about her, though, but some news. I am just pining for a real, choice bit."

She passed the chocolates again. Bess took one, but her sister shook her head.

"Well, as to news," remarked Bess, "we have heard that Sid Wilcox has a new machine."

This was news indeed, after what that youth had said to Cora that very day. Or had he been only fooling her?

"A new one," repeated Cora vaguely, trying to, gather her thoughts.

"Brand, spick—span new," went on Bess. "We haven't seen it, you know, but we've heard that it is a beauty."

"What extravagance!" murmured Cora,—still busily thinking. "His runabout isn't very old. I wonder where he gets all his money?"

"Don't you remember he said he had some to invest in the new issue of bank stock?" suggested Belle.

"But the bank wouldn't let him subscribe," added her sister.

"What did he do with his other car—the one that was broken in the collision?" asked Cora.

"Maybe he—pawned it," suggested Belle, who had rather vague ideas concerning pawnshops.

"Very likely he would if he could." This from Cora with a light laugh. "I guess Sid is very fond of a change—and excitement." She thought of her experience with him.

"Even a change of girls," commented Belle.

"Aula Allen told me that he and Ida were 'on the outs.'"

"Indeed!" and Cora raised her pretty eyebrows. "I fancied he was too—too convenient a friend for Ida to drop. But my dears, as our English teacher says, I have something more important to discuss than Ida Giles and Sidney Wilcox. I'm going to have a 'doings,' as I used to call them."

"Goody!" exclaimed Bess, helping herself to some more of the chocolates. "Make it a lawn party."

"Well, that's just what I want you to help me with. I know that Belle will want to make it a séance with relaxed robes and collapsed masks and relapsed—"

"Oh, you're mean!" exclaimed the taunted one. "I'm not such a freak as that."

"Oh, no," drawled Bess.

"Cer-tain-ly not," added Cora in a teasing tone.

"Well, go on with your 'doings,'" insisted Belle. "I won't make a single suggestion."

"Not make them; but veto them," persisted Cora. "Well, then, never mind, sissy. You sometimes have splendid ideas, even if they are all sterilized."

"And when they are disclosed the sterilization gets away," put in Bess. "That's what mother's nurse declared when we tried on those aprons that come in air-tight packages. But now, Cora, let's have a lawn party."

"Wouldn't it be nicer to have an out-door play?" asked Belle, who had forgotten her resolution not to make a suggestion.

"Oh, dear! I suppose we'll have to have it in the afternoon, when our nurses can be with us," said Bess. "We're supposed to be such kiddies—not out yet, and all that. It's detestable—"

"Indeed," interrupted Cora, "mother says I may have an evening affair, and also out of doors, if I like. Since my last birthday I've been wonderfully grown up."

"Out of doors! And after dark!" cried Bess. "That's great!" and she clapped her hands. "Oh, let's have it a masked affair. I never have been to one in all my life, and I'm just dying to mask!"

"Now, girls, let's be serious," suggested Cora, "for I haven't any too much time to arrange this affair. We ought to have it in June, when we can depend on having a pleasant evening. Suppose we plan a masked mythology fête? Have a dark, green cavern, presided over by: er—um—let's see—who was the gentleman who had charge of passing shades from earth to some place, and where did he pass 'em to?"

"You mean Charon," said Belle. "But, Cora Kimball, do you suppose we could make mythological frocks that would stand damp, night air? Of course, they would be comfortable."

"Oh, we'll manage somehow. At any rate, we'll have a masked 'doin',' that's settled."

"That's all that really counts," said Bess.

"Masks?" questioned Cora. "Just mask in order to be of some account? Not the blessed boys, and the jealous girls—and the chances of pretending you mistake Jack for Walter—and you say a lot of things you are just dying to say, and would not dare to say if you weren't masked. All that—But hush! Here comes Jack!"

"Hello, girls," greeted her brother, and at the sight of Jack, Bess and Belle adjusted themselves in more conventional attitudes. "How are you all?" he went on. "Sis, here's a letter for you. I kept it in my hand all the way from the post-office so as not to forget to give it to you."

"Awfully kind of you, Jack."

Cora glanced at the postmark, and slipped the missive into the large, loose sleeve of her gown.

"Oh, you may read it," spoke Bess, smiling frankly at Jack. "We don't mind."

"Not in the least," came from Jack as he took a chair next to Isabel. "In fact, we would be glad to have you do so. Go ahead, sis. Help yourself," he went on pleasantly, dipping into the chocolate box.

"It will keep," said Cora quickly. "But, Jack, what's new? For mercy's sake, do tell us something new! Is there anything more about—"

"Yes, a lot about it," and Jack anticipated his sister's question. "I hear that the sleuths have a straight tip. They told Ed this afternoon that they would have his money back inside of a—"

"Oh, isn't that fine!" broke in Belle. "I have been so uncomfortable ever since that affair happened and they found the empty wallet in poor, dear Cora's car. It looked just as if we—"

"Don't!" spoke Cora quickly in a low voice.

"It certainly was uncomfortable," put in Bess.

"Especially for Ed Foster," remarked Jack with a. significant grin as he took another chocolate. "Um—um—these are mighty fine, sis!"

"Oh, take them all!" cried Cora. "But tell us some more about it; do, Jack, please!"

"Yes. Do they really think they're on the right track?" asked Isabel.

"That's all I know about it," answered Jack calmly as he finished the last candy. "I heard the detectives had promised to get the money back inside of a week, and that's all. Maybe it was only talk. They have to say something for their pay, you know. But I almost forgot. There is another bit of news, girls."

"What?" they demanded in chorus.

"Ed says he knows who took the money."

As Jack made this announcement he looked around as indifferently as if he had made the most ordinary remark on the most commonplace subject.

CHAPTER XVI

MARY'S LETTER

For a moment there was silence. Then Cora asked:

"Who does he say took it?"

"That's just it," went on her brother. "He doesn't say."

"Does he know?"

"He declares he does."

"Then why won't he tell?"

"You can search me. I don't know. He hasn't even told the police, I understand. He merely made that remark to Walter, and I heard about it."

"Oh, Jack, are you sure that's all there is to it?" asked his sister.

"Sure. I'd tell you more if I knew."

At first they thought he was teasing, and the girls, with, all the wiles of which they were capable, besought him to explain, but he could not, and, finally, they accepted his word as final.

"Well, it's very strange," commented Cora. "I hope it will be all cleared up soon—for all our sakes."

"So do I," joined in Belle.

Cora again referred to the proposed purchase of a car for the twins, and though they were disappointed that they could not have it at once, Cora was rather glad, as she felt it would be a chance for Paul to get the order. Jack was appealed to, and gave the two sisters so many points about autos that they declared they felt quite bewildered.

"Well, I think we'd better be leaving, Cora, dear," said Elizabeth at length, and the good-bys were said, with many whispered promises made to come over the next day to finish up the party plans.

"Cora," said Jack, when the pretty twins had gone down the path, "I want a chance to talk to you. You've been so busy of late that I haven't had an opportunity."

"In just a minute, Bud," interrupted his sister, feeling in her sleeve for the unread letter. "I must run upstairs for just a moment. Then I'll be right down."

"Yes, and then some one else will come in, and it will be the same thing over tomorrow. No, sis, you're not treating me right," and Jack's tone betrayed some grievance.

But Cora decided that she must read her letter, and she promised that she would soon return to the porch.

"I know it's from Mary Downs," she told herself as she glided up the stairs to the privacy of her oven room. "And I never could read it before any one."

She hastily tore open the envelope. Yes, the letter was signed with Mary's name, and it was dated from Silver Falls.

Cora's heart beat expectantly. She had hoped, ever since the day of the eventful ride, that Mary might be able to furnish some clue to the missing money. She was such an observing girl. Cora began to read the letter. It ran:

"*My dear miss Kimball*: I was so sorry to leave you without having a chance to thank you for the pleasant time you gave me, but I was called away unexpectedly that same afternoon. It would only bore you to hear all the details. I simply had to come here, and here I am still. It was most unfortunate, for Madam Julia will never forgive me, and even to her I dislike to tell the reason for the hurried trip. In fact, I think she would not understand it. Well, enough about that.

"I just want to thank you for the lovely time you gave me, and I am so sorry I cannot talk with you, for I have read of the loss of Mr. Foster's money, and surely it was a very strange thing to happen. If I had a chance I might be able to give you a clue but it would not be wise to write it. I expect to be back in Chelton soon, and then I will tell you what I think about it, for I know I can trust you.

"With kindest regards,

"*MaryDowns.*

"P.S.—I was greatly surprised yesterday to meet Mr. Wilcox,

or, rather, to see him pass in a new automobile. He did not see me. I did not want him to.
M. D."

"Of all things!" exclaimed Cora, dropping the letter into her lap. "Just like every other girl on earth. Tells you what she wants you to know, but never says a word about what you want to find out. I've a good mind to let Jack read this letter. He might know what would be best to do."

Then she hesitated. Cora always did hesitate before taking an important step, just as she always stopped and looked around when leaving her room—to see if she had forgotten anything, or if she had left it all right.

"But it does look strange," she reasoned. "Yet I would trust Mary. She has such an honest face. I will just tell Jack the whole thing."

Picking up the letter she hurried back to the porch.

There sat Walter Pennington and Ed Foster with her brother. Concealing one expression of surprise, and another of disappointment that Jack was not alone, Cora greeted the young men pleasantly and invited them in to dinner, an invitation which Jack, in his rough-and-ready fashion had given by asking his chums to stay to dine.

Mrs. Kimball was preparing for a little trip, and though very busy she warmly greeted her son's friends, and entertained them, as she knew so well how to.

"You young folks are so taken up with your motors," she said as she took her place at the head of the table, "that we older and less fortunate people scarcely get a chance to speak to you. Cora is so enthusiastic over her car and its swift motion that our maid declares she will soon turn into a bird and fly."

"A dove," whispered Walter, just loud enough to be heard by every one, but softly enough to disguise the platitude.

Cora laughed lightly. Walter had a very taking way of saying things. He seemed to know exactly how to be nice without being silly.

The dinner over, the young people went to the porch. Mary's letter was in Cora's belt, and the edge of the envelope, scratching her hand as she sat down reminded her of her anxiety concerning the contents. Should she tell all the boys? Ed ought to know, that was her first thought. Surely Jack ought to know of it, and, as for Walter—well, he ought to know also, for he had found the empty pocketbook.

Ed was making some remark to Jack about the lost money. Cora listened to see if it had any reference to what her brother had told her that morning. She crushed the letter in her hands.

"I've just had a note," she began, "from my friend Mary Downs."

"What I From the pretty runaway?" exclaimed Jack. "So that letter was from her, eh? No wonder I didn't recognize the hand."

"She did not run away, Jack," objected his sister, and there was a warning note in her voice.

"Oh, no, of course not. But, anyway, she vas pretty. Wasn't she, boys?"

"A hummer!" declared Walter, adjusting a porch steamer chair for Cora.

"Well, if you want to hear about the letter—" began the girl.

"Hear about it? Why, we want to read it for ourselves!" cried Jack, and he tried to take it from his sister's hand. Cora struggled to retain it, and finding that she was being bested, threw it over Jack's head to Walter. He grabbed it, and defied his chum to touch it.

"Now, easy, fellows," begged Ed in his quiet way. "If there happens to be news from Mistress Mary, though she be quite contrary, pray let us hear it."

"That's what I say," added Walter, handing Cora the missive. "Now, Jack, I'm going to stand on guard, and if you interfere again—"

"Oh, go ahead. I'll get it, anyway, later, when sis is asleep."

"No, you'll not!" declared his sister. "But this is the news," she went on guardedly. "Mary intimates that she knows something about the money."

"Is that so?" cried Ed eagerly.

"Oh, every one is intimating that," declared Jack in some contempt. "Is that all? What we want is an intimation that makes good, eh, Ed?"

"Yes, I suppose so. But what does Mary say?" and he looked sharply at Cora.

"I think I had better read the letter," she said, "for, like all girls, or most of them, at least, she only hints at the most important statement."

"Go ahead," ordered Jack. "I'll listen and close my eyes to call up a picture of pretty Mary. She's pretty, she's witty, she's all a girl—"

He began to sing.

Cora jumped up.

"If any one wants to hear this letter he has got to keep—" she began.

"I'll be good," promised Jack contritely.

Walter gently slipped his arm around Cora's waist. Ed, towering above Walter, put his arm around his chum and Jack's sister. Jack managed to edge under her arm.

"Well, we're a happy family now," said Jack. "You may read the letter, Cora. We each have you all to ourselves."

With a quick move Cora freed herself.

"Oh, you might know she'd duck," pouted Jack, "just as we were getting comfortable. Keep your old letter. I won't listen to it now," and he moved away.

"I've forgotten something in my machine!" exclaimed Ed suddenly with a sly wink at Cora. "I'll just run and get it, if you'll excuse me."

Cora knew exactly what he intended to do. Quickly, as he came back in his runabout, she ran down the piazza steps, and was in the machine before either Walter or Jack realized what was taking place.

"Now I'll hear the letter without being interrupted!" exclaimed Ed as he put on speed and escaped with the laughing girl, who waved the missive above her head.

CHAPTER XVII

A RUNAWAY AUTO

When Cora finished reading Mary's letter to Ed, which did not take long, she looked up at him and asked:

"Well, what do you think of it?"

"I—er—I think—would you mind very much if I didn't tell you what I think of it?" he answered her in turn.

"No," she said slowly; "not if you don't care to. But I thought perhaps—Jack says you know who took the money," she finished hurriedly. She had wanted to get alone with Ed more to ask him this than to read Mary's letter to him.

Ed started.

"Jack said that?" he asked, obviously to gain time.

"Yes."

"I didn't exactly say, that. I said I had my suspicions. He must have misunderstood me."

"Very likely. Jack's rather impetuous. Then you don't know?"

"Not exactly."

"I'll not ask you whom you suspect," declared Cora, though it was hard work not to, for she had her share of curiosity, and she felt, in a measure, that suspicion for the robbery was upon her and her friends.

They were both rather sober after that, and following a short ride around quiet streets Ed brought her home. Walter and Jack were gone.

"Good-by," said Ed as he started away. "If I—er—if I make my suspicions a certainty I'll tell you before I do any one else."

"Will you—really?"

"Yes."

When the Robinson girls called on Cora the next afternoon she had about completed her plans for the lawn fête. It was to be a novel affair, and almost all the eligible young folks of Chelton were to be invited.

"All," declared Cora, "except Sid Wilcox. He simply shall not come."

"But how can you leave him out?" questioned Bess. "Especially as you are going to ask Ida and others in that set."

"I simply will not have him," insisted Cora, "and I don't care what any one thinks about it. He is too—too impertinent to be polite, and I will not run the risk of having him offend some one."

Secretly Cora was thinking of his last transgression, and it afforded her no small consolation to note that her particular friends had not heard of the stolen ride.

Belle, "relaxing" on the low divan in the library window, just where the sun could help her out on the rest theory, was too deeply buried in thought to make rash comment on Cora's decision. She wanted everything simply perfect, and to shape plans with such precision was no easy matter.

"Of course,—you will ask the Sheldons," she finally venture.

"Of course," answered Cora. "But, Belle, we expected a more important remark after such forethought on your part."

"And the Winters," went on the serene one, not noticing the bit of sarcasm.

"Yes; and I have a new star," said Cora quickly. "Who ever do you imagine she can be?"

"I know," declared Bess. "She is Paul's sister."

"Who told you?" demanded Cora.

"Not a soul," Bess assured her; "but I saw you out in your car with her this morning. Isn't she nice."

"Very. But being nice is not her strongest point. She is —brainy."

"O-h-h-h!" sighed Bess. "Then let's not take her up. Belle has brains enough for one town."

"But Hazel isn't that kind. Isn't that a pretty name?" demanded Cora quickly. "She has a different sort of brains. She is a student of nature—biology and evolution, to be exact."

"Perhaps she could tell what makes Bess so—so fat," suggested Belle with marked sarcasm.

"Or what makes you so thin," retaliated Bess.

"At any rate, she is a very sweet girl," declared Cora, "and I'm most anxious for you to meet her. At the same time I am afraid you will like her a lot better than you do me."

"Cora Kimball!" exclaimed Bess. "As if any one could be more likable than you—to us!"

"Oh, I don't know," sighed Cora. "There's Jack."

"Well—er—he's nice—just because he's your brother," replied Bess a bit awkwardly.

"Now for plans," said Cora suddenly, wishing to change the subject, as it was becoming too personal. "We must get the cards out to-morrow. Every one must be masked—that's settled—and we'll try to confine the characters to—"

"The Roman period," interrupted Belle. "That will make it pretty."

"I wonder how the boys will take it?" asked Bess. "I shouldn't wonder if they all came as gladiators."

"Or some such character as Nero," added Belle.

"As long as they don't try to emulate him on his burning Rome affair," came from Cora.

"And every one must keep his or her costume a secret," went on Belle, who was nervous with enthusiasm. "I am not even going to let Bess know whit mine will be."

"All right, sister," replied Bess, glancing at her tiny, enameled watch; "but pray don't be too—too spirituelle. That is, if there were any Roman spirits."

"There was Roman punch!" laughed Cora merrily. "I believe I would like to be Roman punch, if it's not too strong."

"And served up to—" began Bess.

"The gentleman with whom she was riding yesterday afternoon," finished Belle. "The idea of a young lady going out motoring in a morning dress—"

"Bareheaded," chimed in Bess, and a laugh followed.

"Come to think of it, girls," spoke Cora, making an effort to get back to the party, "I do not think we ought to confine this fête to any particular period. Suppose some one wants to be—well, say, Priscilla—and has been wanting to be Priscilla all her life."

"That's right," agreed Bess. "It's just like you, Cora, to think all around a thing. Yes, I vote for a masked fête. Any sort of a costume, so long as we are masked."

Belle also agreed that this would be a better plan than the one first proposed, and then the trio of girls busied themselves over the invitation list. There was no time to spare, as the "doings" must come off before Mrs. Kimball's trip to Bermuda, for which she was preparing.

"And you feel you must invite Ida?" asked Bess. "I am sure she is almost as certain to do something rude as Sid would be."

"Yes, we had better have her," declared Cora, putting down Ida's name on the long list. "Ida is not really mean—she is rather unfortunate—and I think, as she has been in Chelton so long it would be unkind to leave her out."

"I hardly think she will come," commented Belle. "She has been so—so snippy lately."

"Well, we'll ask her, at any rate. And, now, don't forget, we are all to keep our costumes secret."

"Oh, won't it be jolly!" sang out Bess. "I can scarcely wait."

"And to think of having it after dark, without chaperons to look after us!" exclaimed Belle. "I doubt if some of the stiff girls will be allowed to come on that account."

"Then we'll have a better time without the stiffs," declared the young hostess. "I'm sure our patronesses are protection enough, and mother is going to delay her trip a few days on purpose to be on hand."

"Oh, of course," Belle hurried to explain, "I think it is just perfectly all right and delicious, but I was just speculating on the kind who may be jealous."

"And is Paul coming?" asked Bess. She was always so self-conscious when she asked a question like that.

"Why, of course," answered Cora, "and also his sister Hazel. I particularly like them both, and Jack, who has met Paul, agrees that he is a very nice young man."

"Expert opinion, I suppose," murmured Belle.

They talked in jolly mood for some time longer, and the twins were about to leave for home when a shout out in the street attracted their attention.

"What's that?" asked Cora, starting up.

"Runaway! Look out for the runaway!" the girls heard several persons shout.

"It's a horse running `away," declared Belle. "Let's stay where it's safe—up here."

But Cora had started down the path, and Bess followed her.

"It's a runaway motor—a car!" exclaimed Cora as she caught sight of something flashing through the trees. It was a runabout, dashing along the avenue without a hand to guide it, and as it gathered speed it swerved from side to side.

"Why, it's Jack's car!" cried Cora as the auto flashed past her. "Can he be hurt? Where is he? 'Oh, Jack!"

She started to run, leaving Bess on the path.

"I must stop it!" thought Cora. "It may run into a person or a team and kill some one."

Before she thought of the uselessness of her act she found herself running down the street, along with a shouting crowd of men and boys. As if she could catch up to an auto!

She hardly knew what she was doing.

"Oh, can't some one stop it?" she cried. "Turn off the power! It must be stopped!"

"By Jove! That's a plucky chap!" exclaimed a stranger. "There! He's lost his hold! He'll be run over!"

A young man, who had made a daring attempt to stop the runabout, was seen to be slipping beneath the wheels. But as the car sped on he pulled himself up to the seat. He grasped the wheel just in time to prevent the car from running up on the sidewalk, and an instant later he had shut off the, power and applied the brakes.

"Why, it's Ed Foster!" exclaimed Cora as she came up beside the halted runabout. "Oh, Ed, are you hurt? I'm, so glad you stopped Jack's car. There might have been a bad accident."

"Oh, I'm all right. I nearly slipped out, though. How did it happen?"

"I don't know. We were sitting on our piazza when we heard the cry, and I saw the car speeding away."

"Where's Jack?"

"I don't know that, either. I'm afraid he's hurt."

"The car doesn't seem to be damaged," remarked a man who had been nearly run down.

The crowd, rather disappointed, on the whole, that no accident had happened, turned away. Cora got in Jack's car beside Ed, who started the machine back. They were met half way to the Kimball home by Paul Hastings.

"Any damage done?" he called out as soon as he saw them. He appeared very anxious.

"None, but it was a narrow squeak," answered Ed.

"Where's Jack?" asked Cora.

"We took him home."

"Oh, is he—is he badly hurt?"

"No; only a sprained leg, I believe, and some bruises. The doctor is there."

"How did it happen?" asked Cora quickly.

"Why, Jack brought his machine to the garage to have a little repairing done. I had finished it, and he and I were in the office talking, when a fellow named Lem Gildy came along and threw in the clutch, starting the car off.'

"Jack saw him do it and ran out, trying to stop his runabout, but he wasn't quick enough, and was knocked down. I hurried out to pick him up, and I forgot all about the runaway car until I had taken Jack home. There was considerable excitement, as there was a brand-new car, a very expensive one, belonging to the Blends, in front of our garage, and the runabout nearly crashed into it. If it had, the new machine would have been wrecked."

"And what became of Lem Gildy?" asked Ed.

"Oh, he sneaked off, after whining out that he didn't mean any harm. But I think he did. He's a suspicious character."

"Hurry home. I want to see Jack," begged Cora.

Ed started Jack's runabout off again, after telling Paul what had happened down the street. The handsome young chauffeur said he would presently call at the house and inquire after Jack.

Cora found her brother in bed, where her mother had insisted that he go, though he declared he was not hurt much. Dr. Dearborn had examined him, and said he would be all right in a few days.

"Oh, weren't you awfully frightened, Cora?" asked Bess, who, with her sister, had remained at the Kimball home.

"Indeed I was, but I knew the car had to be stopped."

"And it was going some," added Ed.

"I can't see what motive Lem would have in starting the car," said Cora. "I never knew him to be malicious—only worthless."

"I believe he planned this," declared Paul, who had just arrived.

"Why so?" asked Cora.

"Well, he's been hanging around the garage for several days past, and numbers of times I've ordered him away. I heard him asking one of the men, the other day, how to throw in a clutch on a car like Jack's, and that made me suspicious."

"But what could his object be?" asked Ed, rubbing one arm, that was strained from his exertion in stopping the car:

"I believe him to be in the pay of some one," declared Paul with flashing eyes, "and I believe his object was to get me into trouble. As I told you, there stood in front of the garage a valuable new car belonging to the Blends. Their chauffeur was about to take it out for a run. If Jack's car, started by Lem, had smashed into it I would have been blamed, for I ran the car out of the garage, for their chauffeur. Then I would have lost my position here, and probably would not get that new one in New City, for the garage people would have blacklisted me."

"Oh, mercy!" gasped Belle. "Wouldn't that have been dreadful!"

"Bad for me," admitted Paul with a smile. "But I'm sorry Jack was hurt."

"Thank goodness it's no worse!" exclaimed Cora. "But, Mr. Hastings, whom do you think paid Lem to do such a mean thing?"

"I'd rather not say," answered the young garage manager. "But I shall keep my ears and eyes open, and if I find out what I suspect to be true—well, there'll be trouble for somebody."

He spoke with flashing eyes, and Cora looked at him admiringly.

"Well, since we know how your brother is, I think we'll be going, Cora," said Bess, and she and her sister took their departure, followed by Paul and Ed.

"I wonder why Lem Gildy did that?" asked Cora of herself as she went to her room that night. "Who is urging him on? Did he want to injure Jack, as well as make trouble for Paul? Well, I'll have to give up thinking of it now," she finished, "but, like Paul—I suppose I ought to say Mr. Hastings—I'm going to keep my eyes and ears on the alert, too."

CHAPTER XVIII

THE GARDEN Fête

It was a perfect evening—the very last of the perfect June days. Chelton lay like a contented babe in Nature's lap—contented, but not asleep, for it was the evening of the masked garden fête.

The bright-colored lanterns throughout the spacious grounds of the Kimball home flickered like eager fireflies, and the splendid dancing platform, erected on the broad lawn, fairly glistened with its coat of wax under the strings of tiny electric lights that canopied the pavilion.

It was not deemed necessary to have any one at the gate. In Chelton there were not many strangers and suppose some urchins did enter, Cora said, it would be a pity to deny them a glimpse of the pretty sight.

A tall Antonio, in a garb of the most somber black, strolled about, hoping to find his Portia. Priscilla was there, in her collar and cap, but where was John Alden? Would the dainty little Bo-peep, who looked like a bisque doll, ever find her straying sheep?

Then motor "togs"—a long linen duster, with a cap and goggles—seemed a most convenient mask for so many young men, who were not vain enough to want to don doublet and hose.

But there were some courtiers, and they did look romantic. Perhaps that stout girl in the white Empire gown, with a baby cap on her head, and a rattler around her neck, might be Bess Robinson.

But the Winter girls were both stout—as stout as Bess. Then that thin creature, so tall that she suggested a section of sugar cane (could she actually be in one piece), might be Belle. The Psyche knot at the back of her head, and the wreath of wild olive, certainly bespoke Belle.

What had Cora done? Whom had she impersonated? There were many who wished to know this, and there were so many pretty persons that very likely she might have taken a very simple character. Cora disliked too much trouble, where trouble did not seem to count.

That splendid figure of Liberty might be she. Or that indolent Cleopatra on the rustic bench under the white birch tree—she made a pretty picture. But Cora would not pose as this one was doing. The vacant seat beside the girl was too glaring an invitation for Cora to offer. Perhaps she might be that suffragette, who went about demanding "Votes for women!" See! There she is now, holding up Marc Anthony!

A most attractive figure was Night or Luna. The coloring would have suited Cora—- the black hair and the silvery trimmings of the robe to represent the moon but it was not like Cora to seek the dark spots of the garden that her moonbeams might be the brighter. The boys had a certain fancy for moonlight—hand made.

"I'll wager you are Bess," whispered a very handsome Adonis in a real Greek costume—all but the pedestal.

"Yes," answered the girl with a titter. "As you please—but, I pray you, fair sir, am I not a good milkmaid?"

"The best ever," replied Adonis. "Pray let us stroll in yonder meadow."

Slipping his hand into the bare arm of the milkmaid, Adonis drew the figure down a pith toward the small lake that was on one edge of the Kimball property.

"Now I have some one to talk to," he declared with evident satisfaction.

"Oh, is that all?" replied the maid in some contempt "I can't see just why I should fill in that way," and she arose from her seat at the water's edge. "Besides," she added, "I hate Greeks. They are so vain!" and with this she hurried after a girl in a nun's costume, who was walking along the path to the pavilion.

"Well!" exclaimed the disappointed youth, "that was hard luck. And just as I was going to say something nice, too. However, it'll keep, I suppose," and he followed the two figures—the nun and the milkmaid—toward the dancing platform.

A veritable Rosebud was bowing on the porch to the row of unmasked patronesses, several ladies of Mrs. Kimball's set, who had volunteered to help her receive.

The Rosebud wore a plaited garb of rose pink, with velvet petals about her waist, and green velvet leaves about her throat. The costume was so beautiful, and the figure so graceful, to say nothing of the natural rose perfume it exhaled, that every one stopped to admire.

The bell for the cotillion sounded, and when the ribbons were cast to the gentlemen it was the Greek Adonis who caught the blue end. He would lead.

For his partner he walked up to the saucy milkmaid, and claiming her by right, proudly marched with her on his arm back to the center of the platform.

A murmur of disapproval was heard. Why had he not chosen Cleopatra?

But Marc Anthony was eagerly waiting, and quickly sprang to the fair charmer's side. Antonio, the silent, strode over to the market woman—the height of incongruity.

A clown somersaulted to the Rosebud.

Night hung back. She seemed particular with whom she danced, and when a very handsomely proportioned courtier stepped up to her she refused him with a toss of her head. A star fell from her black tresses, but the answer seemed final, and the courtier walked away.

Finally the music started, and the dancers with it. How delightful it was to be some one else! And how splendidly Adonis led! At each turn where the waltz varied the figures he effected a wonderful change of partners, and it usually happened just when he was saying something most interesting to the young lady.

But this afforded a splendid chance for coquetry—a very pardonable affectation under a mask.

The little nun was creeping around the platform. She seemed like a dark spirit in the midst of such merrymaking, almost like a warning of a fate to come.

"Now!" the Rosebud heard her partner whisper as the nun passed. And the Rosebud had for a partner—Antonio,

"Who?" Psyche heard the nun ask of the same Antonio. "Who is it to go to?"

Psyche wondered what it meant. With a quick move, at the signal for a change, Antonio was whirling off with the nun, and Psyche was left without a partner.

But a few moments later Antonio came back to her.

"I just wanted to see if I could make the little nun dance," he whispered, "and I did—all the way off the platform, for she's gone."

"She is standing there by the side of Adonis," replied Psyche directly. "And she seems to be in the way."

"Soliciting alms," almost sneered Antonio. "That's her business, I suppose."

Psyche was glad when the waltz ended, and at the next figure she came in contact with Rosebud. It was to be a ladies' bouquet, and Rosebud made the centerpiece, with all the other pretty sprites in a circle about her. Then the boys, in an outer ring, threw their flower-chained hands into the inner circle, thus each capturing a pretty partner.

The milkmaid fell into Antonio's arms. He almost caught her up from the floor.

"Don't!" she objected as she felt his hands on her bare arm. "Your hands are—are too damp. They'll take all the starch out of my sleeves."

"Sign of a warm heart," he answered as he led her away.

Adonis was with Rosebud. What a charming couple they made! And how perfectly they both danced!

Close beside them fluttered Night. She was with the clown and seemed to enjoy the contrast.

One of the most distinguished masculine figures was Hiawatha, the Indian lad. His face was made up with real skill, and his bow and quiver hung gracefully at his back as he strode about. He had not danced, but he was evidently having a most delightful time with the Moon figure and Buttercup.

At the intermission a general onslaught was made by the young men to penetrate the disguises worn by the ladies.

"Plagued awkward," complained Hiawatha when he had failed to ascertain who Luna was. "I might be making love to my own—"

"Sister!" snapped the girl, laughing at the youth's discomfiture.

"But won't you tell me just this?" he pleaded. "Who on earth is the girl in the black robe—the nun? See, there she goes off toward the lake with Antonio."

"How can I tell?" answered Luna. "But if you really want to know, suppose we follow them?"

"Great idea!" agreed the Indian. "There goes Rosebud and Adonis. My, but they are hitting the trail, if you will pardon the language of an early settler. Suppose we go around this way? Then we can have a full view of both pairs in this mystery."

"As you please," answered Luna with some condescension as they started toward the little lake.

"Shall we sit here?"

It was Adonis speaking to Rosebud. She sank down upon a rustic bench and instantly noticed a couple turn behind the spruce hedge.

They were both in black. It was Antonio and the nun.

CHAPTER XIX

A STRANGE DISCOVERY

Adonis and Rosebud sat for a while at the side of the miniature lake, where the pretty little lights dimpled in the placid waters, and where now a score of merrymakers were clamoring for a ride in the tiny launch which Jack Kimball and his chums, Ed and Walter, had rigged up, in order to add picturesqueness to the fête.

"Don't you want to take a sail?" asked the Greek youth of his fair companion.

"Oh, no, indeed, thank you. I must leave that for the others."

"You must?" and he accented the last word, as if to penetrate her disguise by this act of deference to the "others."

"Oh, well," she answered hesitatingly, "I never did care much for sailing, to tell the truth—especially in a—tub. I prefer a place where there is at least room in which to dip my hands."

"Then let us walk," he suggested. "I am anxious to see all over the grounds. Aren't they splendid? Just see that cave formed by the cedars, back of the lighted path. I declare' this place looks like a real fairyland to-night."

"I am glad you like it," replied the girl. "I—er—" She clapped her dainty hand over her masked mouth. She was near to betraying her identity.

"Like it?" he repeated. "How could I do otherwise? But in all this human garden there is no fairer flower than—Rosebud," and he brought her hand reverently to his lips.

"Oh! You—you mustn't be too—too gay!" she expostulated, but she laughed as she said it. "You know the patronesses have specified—"

"There!" he exclaimed, interrupting her. "It's all right, Rosebud," and he tucked her arm within his own. "I will make love to the trees if it pleases you. But let us walk about the grounds. I am afraid the curtain will be suddenly rung down and leave us again just mortals."

Rosebud felt that it was, pretty—very pretty. She was entirely satisfied with herself and her friends. Then Adonis—wasn't he splendid? And how courteous—almost like the brave knights of old.

They approached a spot gloomy with shadows.

From it they heard voices in a gentle murmur—voices near what Adonis had called the cedar cave.

Involuntarily, at the sound of one voice, Rosebud pressed her companion's arm. She heard some one say:

"I must go home at once—I am so frightened!"

There came an answering whisper, but it was in tones that indicated a youth pleading.

"I have—I have done it," again came the girl's frightened whisper. "I did what you asked me to, and I don't see why you don't take me home."

There was almost a sob in her voice.

"What? Just when I'm having a fine time?" objected the other. "Why don't you want to stay? No one could have seen you drop it into——"

"Hush!" cautioned the girl desperately.

"Oh, you're just nervous—that's all."

Rosebud felt that she should not hear any more, but she would either have to cross the path near the cave and allow the hidden ones to see her, or she must wait until they had come out, as, if she and her companion retreated now, they would make a noise on the gravel, and it would be heard. Adonis seemed to understand the situation, and whispered to his companion:

"Stay. They'll be gone in a moment." He drew her farther back into the shadows.

"If you don't take me home," continued the girl in the cedar cave, "I'll ask some one else to. I certainly shall not stay until supper and have to unmask. I dare not."

"Just as you like," was the cool response.

"And I risked it all for you—spoiled my entire evening. I'll know better next time!"

"Well, I'm going to make it up to you," said her companion.

There was a movement of the cedars, and two figures emerged from amid the trees. They crossed the path. They were Antonio and the nun.

Rosebud drew Adonis farther back from the path. The others passed on without seeing them and at once began talking gaily, as if they had been merrymaking with the rest but Rosebud and Adonis detected the false note in their laughter. Adonis pressed the little warm hand on his sleeve.

"Do you know them?" he asked.

"I—suspect them," she replied.

"So do I," he almost gasped, "and with good reason. I have just found something in my pocket."

"In your pocket?"

"Yes, quite a bulky package. I did not notice it until this moment."

"But how—"

"Don't ask me how it got there. It's just—there. I did not even know there was a pocket in this cloak I wore. Whoever put the package there was more clever than I."

"But what is it?"

"I'm going to look—Cora."

"Cora? Then you know me—Ed?"

"As you do me. Of course. Did you think you could deceive me?"

"I—I hoped to. But the package—what does, it contain?"

"We will look—together."

He led her to a dangling electric light, drew, something from the folds of his cloak, and unwrapped the paper. Then he gave an exclamation of surprise.

"Ten thousand dollars of my missing bonds!" he whispered.

"Really, Ed?"

He extended them to her.

"Oh, Ed! I'm so glad!"

"So am I, yet I have been suspecting it."

"Suspecting it?"

"Yes. I may as well admit it, of late I have not worried about my loss. Recently I have been convinced that it would come back. And you see I was right."

"But this is only half of it."

"I know, but the rest will come. It is not so easy to return the cash."

"But who could have slipped it into your pocket?"

"Don't you know? Can't you guess—after what we heard?"

"The—the nun?"

"Exactly."

"And she is—"

"That is a mystery—as yet, but I have my suspicions. She brushed past me in a crowd, and I thought I felt her hand upon my velvet cloak, but as I never suspected the garment contained a pocket, I gave it no further thought. Had I the remotest idea—what had happened there might have been a disturbance. But the talk we heard just now gave me a clue."

"Hush!" exclaimed Cora, and she shivered slightly in her rather thin costume. "Here come Paul and Belle. I have penetrated their disguises. Isn't Paul splendid as Marc Anthony? and Belle makes a perfectly classical Psyche."

"And Walter?" asked Ed with a veiled hint of jealousy in his tones.

"It was horrid of him to play the clown."

"But I like him best in some such humble rôle," spoke Ed.

"I wish you had not discovered me," went on Cora. "It would be such fun to hear things, and say things, in some other character than ourselves."

"But I could not find, even in the Rosebud, a fairer type than that of Jack's real sister," he replied gallantly.

"There's the supper gong!" exclaimed Cora; "and I must hurry away, as I have my duties to look after. Oh, but I'm so glad about the money. I wish it were all back. Are you going to make this public?"

"I don't know. We'll talk about it again."

"Well, run along now," commanded the girl with a pretty air of superiority. "Why don't you join in with that milkmaid and Pocahontas? They are charming—both of them."

"I think I will just run along with—Rosebud," he answered, and he drew her arm more firmly within his own as they advanced toward the fairy tables set about all over the lawn, where, as the repast was served, masks were suddenly taken off, and the merrymakers were treated to many surprises.

"Oh!" cried the pretty milkmaid to Hiawatha. "How could you—Jack Kimball?"

"Oh!" answered Jack, who had quite recovered from his little auto accident. "Oh! How could you—Bess? And you know perfectly well you did squeeze my hand—once."

"Oh, you horrid boy, I did not!"

"Well, you may now, if you like," and he extended it, but Bess drew back.

"And to think," cried the beautiful Psyche, who was Belle Robinson, "that I have actually been—"

"Letting a perfectly strange chap make love to you!" added Paul, helping her out, for Paul was Marc Anthony, and had spent considerable time with Belle.

"Oh!" cried the girl, recovering herself quickly. "Was that— making—love?" and she looked archly at him.

"I—er—I rather hoped it was," he replied grimly.

Night—Hazel, you must know—had been flitting around with Hiawatha and the clown, but toward the end the latter had attached himself to her, to the exclusion of the Indian youth, and now Walter Pennington, with a shake of his head which set all the foolish little bells to ringing, told Paul's sister how delighted he was to renew his acquaintance with her.

Adonis and Rosebud had a table directly under the umbrella tree.

"I must run in-doors for a second," Cora whispered to Ed when the ices were being passed. "I want to speak to Jack. I just saw him going in."

"May I come?"

"With me?"

"Yes. You see, those bonds are burning a hole in well, in my lace handkerchief, and I wish Jack would put them in the safe in the house."

"Why, certainly. Come along. But see, there is Antonio—and the nun is not with him."

"Yes," spoke Ed. "I saw her go away with Priscilla."

"Priscilla?"

"Yes; and John Alden never spoke for himself."

"Priscilla," murmured Cora. "Do you know who she was?"

"No. Who?"

"Mary Downs."

"Mary—why, I thought she was out of town."

"She was, but she came back to-day, and I helped her fix up a costume. And so the nun went off with her?"

Cora walked slowly toward the house, Ed following.

CHAPTER XX

THE AFTERMATH

Ed Foster and Jack Kimball sat in the library of the latter's home until quite late that night—long after the merrymakers had departed.

"If you suspect who put the bonds into your pocket," Jack was saying, "don't you think the easiest way to clear it up would be directly to accuse the suspect?"

"No," answered Ed, "for I feel that it will all come out shortly, without any unnecessary publicity. You see, the money and bonds may only have been—er—well, let's say borrowed. Just as many banks are robbed. Or the person who took it may have thought there was only a small sum in the wallet, and finding such a large one, probably became terribly frightened, and did not know what to do."

"Well, of course it's your affair," returned Jack and looked thoughtful, "but, in a measure, it affects my sister."

"It never did affect your sister, Jack, and never can. I am sorry about the wallet being found in her car, but there never was the most remote—"

"Oh, I know, of course not, on your part. But others—"

"No one ever really suspected her. And, what is more, I have it from her own lips that she would rather not have the guilty ones punished, for she thinks, as I do, that the money and bonds were not taken as a deliberate robbery."

"Well, what are you going to do—wait?"

"Yes. I shall invest these bonds so they will be safe, and then let time do the rest. I do not think we shall have long to wait. They have been holding the bank stock for me, so I have not really suffered—thus far."

"Well, you certainly are a cool one!" complimented Jack. "If I thought some one had my money—some coward, as this person must be, to keep silent all this while—I would never sleep until I had it back."

Ed smiled rather indulgently and indifferently.

"Well, you see," he went on, "I have gotten along so many years without the use of that twenty thousand dollars that I did not miss it when it was taken. Of course, I am losing interest on it, but I can easily make that up."

"Then suppose we retire?" suggested Jack, for Ed was to be his guest for the remainder of the night. "I am actually sweltering in these togs. Aren't you in a hurry to get back into yourself and be just Ed Foster?"

"No; I rather like being Adonis. I fancy I like him infinitely more than I cotton to that Foster chap," and he laughed.

"Well, you made a hit," complimented Jack.

"Thanks."

Ed stood up and surveyed himself in a pier glass. He laughed at the figure he presented, but there was a serious look upon his handsome face. Fancy Adonis being serious!

"You also made good, Jack," he said after a pause. "I don't know when I've seen a braver brave. Do you ever expect to get that stuff off your face in time to go back to college?"

"I guess it will wear off. If it doesn't I'll use gasolene from the auto tank, or take a steam bath at some lady beauty doctress's establishment." He rubbed his countenance vigorously with his handkerchief. "If it doesn't remove," he added, "I'll tell 'em I've got the jaundice."

"Did you see Sid this evening?" asked Ed.

"I thought I saw him, and then I wasn't sure. He wasn't invited. Whom do you think he was?"

"I—well, I wouldn't be sure, either," answered Ed evasively. "I saw so many chaps about his size and build that it was hard to distinguish. Hastings was splendid, wasn't he? I like that fellow."

"So do I. He's perfectly square, and measures up all right. I managed to get the order for the Robinson twins' auto for him."

"You did?"

"Yes. You know, he is going to represent the Whitehall automobile concern from the first of the month, over in New City. Going to take one of their cars across country, you know. He was mighty pleased to get the order. It was Cora's idea, of course. She is just full of such ideas—always thinking of other people."

"That's right. She never does lose a chance to do a fellow a good turn. I suppose she told you about the ride when she and Paul outdid Sidney Wilcox?"

"No; but Paul did. Wasn't that plucky of her?" and Jack beamed with admiration. "Cora has a lot more courage than have some fellows I know."

"Indeed she has," and Ed's voice was earnest.

The tall clock was chiming two when the young men left the library. They had so many things in common that they talked like two girls. Just as they passed the hall door they were startled by a quick step on the veranda.

"Hello! Who's that?" asked Jack, hurrying to the portal.

"It's me—Paul Hastings," answered a voice outside, and as Jack swung open the door the young chauffeur, who was still in his costume, entered. He seemed greatly excited.

"I was afraid you'd be in bed," he panted, "and I ran until I'm all out of breath."

"But what's the matter?" asked Ed.

"Come on in and sit down," invited Jack. "We're not particular whether we go to bed or sit up the rest of the night. Come and join us. But has anything happened?"

"No; I—I can't stay," and Paul leaned against the doorway. "But I found this in my coat pocket—it's a diamond ring. I was nearly home when I discovered it. I thought some of the girls or ladies might be frantic over the loss, so I hurried back with it."

He handed over the sparkling object.

"Whew! That's a beauty!" exclaimed Jack. "A new one, too! Look, Ed! If that isn't an engagement ring I'll eat my war club! Now, what young lady, do you suppose, could have used our grounds, our hospitality and eaten of our swell supper with the malicious aforethought of becoming pledged to unite herself in the holy bonds of matrimony? Who could have done it? And then to lose the guarantee that goes with it! It's past belief!"

"It certainly is new," said Ed, critically examining the ring with its sparkling stone. "About a carat and a half, I should say. Never cost less than three hundred dollars. Whoever bought it must have plenty of cash. But how on earth did it get into your pocket, Paul?"

Ed was rapidly thinking of something that had happened to him that nigh.

"That's what gets me," replied Paul. "Of course, these costume rigs are full of holes and corners. A girl might have been dancing with me, and the ring may have slipped from her finger into my pocket. Perhaps it was too large for her, being new. But I did not notice that I danced with any one wearing it."

"Still, it might have happened that way," admitted Jack, "especially if she kept the stone turned in so no one, would see it. That's a trick they have."

"At any rate, she is sure to come back here for it," went on Paul, "and I wanted to save her any possible anxiety. I hope it belongs to some real nice girl, and if it does, don't forget to say that I found it. And you might add that I would be glad to receive a small reward in the shape of permission to show the aforesaid pretty girl the sights around here in the auto I am soon to run."

"All right," laughed Jack. "That would be some sort of reward. But, as for myself, I must confess I would prefer a smile of gratitude. Just fancy the girl receiving back her ring! Won't she flop over in a sheer state of collapse!"

"Have you looked inside the ring?" asked Ed. "There might be a name or initials in it."

"Never thought of it," admitted Paul. "Hazel, who was with me when I found it, made me hurry right back, and I didn't get a chance."

Jack lead the circlet, and holding it close to a drop-light, he peered closely at it.

"By Jove!" he exclaimed. "There are initials!"

"Whose?" asked Ed.

"'I.G.' Whose are they? 'I.G.' Why, of course. `I.G.'—Ida Giles! Whoever would have thought it? Ida Giles with an engagement ring!"

"And why not?" queried Ed. "Isn't Ida the bright-red, dashing sort? Lots of fellows would call her dashing, and, from what I have seen of her to-night, she certainly is bright."

"Well, of all things!" exclaimed Jack, who seemed unable to get over it. "And you're on her side, eh, Ed? Why, man, not a fellow in the whole of Chelton ever got through more than one dance with her—except Sid Wilcox, and I can't see why he sticks to her."

"Then the Chelton fellows are slow," commented Ed as he critically examined the ring. "I think Ida is quite taking."

"Was she here to-night?" asked Paul.

"She was invited," replied Jack, "for I saw her name on one of the bids Cora sent out. But I did not have the pleasure of a personal interview with her this evening, and so I can't say whether she was here or not."

"Well," remarked Paul, moving toward the door, "I guess I'll be leaving again. Take care of the ring, Jack, and don't forget to give the lady who calls for it my regards. And say, Jack, please thank your sister for me for getting the order for that car for the Robinsons. I'm going after it to-morrow morning—no, I mean this morning. It's after three o'clock now."

"Oh, I'm sure Cora was only too glad to be able to get you the chance."

"And thank you, also. I know the part you had in it."

"Oh, I didn't do anything. It was all Cora. Though of course Bess Robinson would deny me nothing," added Jack and laughed. "She thinks I'm simply perfect. I heard her tell Cora so," and Jack walked up and down in pretended self-admiration, while the others threatened to pick him up and toss him out into the cold moonlight, where they said he belonged in that particular state of lunacy.

"Ida's ring," mused Jack, after he had calmed down. "Just plain Ida. Now if it had only been Bess, Belle or—Hazel."

"No, no!" protested Paul.

"Well, all right," assented Jack. "Ida's it is." He wrapped the ring carefully in paper and put it in his pocket. "I'll take the best of care of it, Paul, of course, and I'll also collect the reward for you, and hand it over personally. You can trust me for that. But I wonder why we haven't had some inquiries from Ida before this?"

"Maybe she is so unused to it that she hasn't missed it," suggested Ed.

"No girl is ever unused to her first engagement ring," declared Paul. "Well, I'm going. Goodnight."

"This finding of things in pockets is growing interesting," remarked Ed when the door had closed on Paul. "I wonder if any of the girls found valuables in their costumes?"

"Hardly," declared Jack. "No one could ever find their pockets to drop anything in. But I'll put this in the safe and mark it `to be kept until called for.' Won't Cora and the other girls be surprised!" and he slammed the iron door shut, having, by an odd chance, dropped the diamond circlet into the very compartment that contained the bonds so strangely returned to Ed.

127

CHAPTER XXI

REAL MOTOR GIRLS

Cora was up early the next morning, and went out alone for a spin in her car. She wanted to think over the happenings at the lawn fête, to recall various matters, and to try to straighten out some tangles that confused her. It was delightful to skim along the quiet road, the powerful motor of her car singing a song of speed and progress.

"I suppose Jack and Ed are sleeping yet," she said to herself, "though how Ed can, after the strange recovery of his bonds, is more than I can understand."

Ed was gone when she returned, and Jack seemed surprised to see his sister returning from an early morning run.

"I thought you'd sleep for hours yet," he said "I've got something to tell you."

"Is it about the bonds?"

"No, not exactly. Look at that!"

He held out the diamond ring.

"Jack!" she cried with a little catch in her voice. "You don't mean to tell me that's an engagement Ting?"

"That's exactly what it is."

"But for some girl—"

"Of course it's for a girl," answered her brother, seeing that his sister was under a misapprehension, and not being able to resist the chance to tease her. "Of course it's for a girl. And—"

"Oh! But Jack, what will mother say—you becoming engaged—"

"Who said I was engaged?" he asked. "Look inside and you'll see whose it is."

"Ida Giles!" cried Cora.

"Exactly. She lost it," and to end her increasing wonder, Jack told his sister the circumstances.

Cora wanted to go at once and return the ring to Ida, but Jack said:

"No, we'll wait for her to call. If she wants it very much she'll come."

"But why don't you want me to give it to her?"

"Well, I'll tell you some other time," and with that evasive answer Cora had to be content.

Several days passed, and Ida did not come, but Jack would not consent to Cora returning the ring to her. In the meanwhile the young people had discussed over and over again the beautiful fête given by Cora, though the finding of the bonds and the story of the ring was kept within a small, select circle. Ed Foster took the bonds to the bank and received for them part of the stock for which he had negotiated. The rest, he said, would be held for him.

"And I'm pretty sure I'll get the rest of my twenty thousand dollars back soon," he said. "At least, nearly all the cash."

Mrs. Kimball went to the city to prepare for her trip to Bermuda, and it was a few days later, when some of the recent excitement had worn off, that Cora began to feel a sense of loneliness stealing over her. Her mother seldom went away from home.

"Oh, dear!" she exclaimed as she sat in the library trying to be interested in a book. "I wish something—"

Out on the driveway a triumphant "honk-honk!" drew her attention.

"I hope that's—" she began, but she did not finish, for she saw the Robinson twins in a shining, new car, Bess at the wheel, as though she had been running one for months, and the sisters both attired in their becoming motoring costumes.

"Come on!" cried Bess as Cora leaned out of the window. "Get your car and we'll take a spin! Isn't ours a beauty?"

"Oh, isn't it!" cried Cora delightedly. "But I thought it wasn't to come for a week."

"We couldn't help deceiving you, Cora, dear," answered Belle. "But you see—"

"And you can run it all alone?" interrupted Cora.

"Yes, all by our lonelies," answered Bess. "You see, we wanted to surprise you, so we didn't tell you exactly when it was coming. When it arrived we got Paul—I mean Mr. Hastings, of course—we got him to give us lessons along a quiet road, where we never met any one who knew us. And father is not a bit timid about us going out alone since Paul—I mean—"

"Never mind explaining," broke in Cora with a laugh.

"Well, since Paul showed us how to run it. Papa has taken a great notion to Paul," finished Bess with the suspicion of a blush.

"How about the daughter?" asked Cora gaily. "Of course, she would never take a notion to the same young man her father happened to favor."

"Oh, you horrid creature!" exclaimed Bess. "He did teach me beautifully, of course. But a girl may look at a chauffeur, I suppose, just as a cat may gaze at a crowned monarch."

"Oh, certainly," conceded Cora. "So you are really going out for a spin? I'll get ready and we'll go together: I was just wondering what I could do until dinner-time. Jack is out with some friends, and I was just plain lonesome."

"Put on your new costume," directed Belle. "We want people to look at us. Isn't it perfectly splendid to have a regular set of cars?"

"Yes. We ought to get up an auto show," agreed Cora as she hastened off to make ready for her ride.

They selected a quiet road. In spite of the shadows of the trees it was hot. The swift motion of the cars, however, relieved the humidity of the atmosphere in a measure.

"Which way?" asked Cora as they came to a turn.

"Down by the river," suggested Bess. "We haven't been out Woodbine way all summer. Let's go this afternoon."

"All right. I guess I'll let you set the pace," answered Cora as she held her car back and allowed Bess to take the lead, which the fair amateur motorist did gracefully and with no little skill.

They attracted some attention as they skimmed along in their new outfits and their new cars, And with their bright faces showing their happiness.

Many stopped to look and admire and could not but smile at the evident pleasure the motor girls were having.

"'Far from the maddening crowd,'" quoted Belle as they swung down the quiet river road. "But do be careful, Bess," she urged. "I know you understand as much about the car as I do, but I always feel that I ought to have a life preserver on when any mere girl—including myself—is at the helm of such a powerful craft."

Bess laughed and replied lightly. She had perfect confidence in her ability to guide the Flyaway, as they had christened the new car.

"Isn't it close?" called Cora as she tried to steer out of the way of a stone and failed, thereby receiving quite a jolt. "I'm afraid we're going to have rain before we get back—a thunder shower, likely. It's sultry."

"Oh, I hope we don't have a storm," replied Bess. "I'll hate to get my new machine all splashed up with mud, to say nothing of spoiling our new auto suits."

"Then we had better not get too far out and away from shelter," suggested Cora. "There! Isn't that thunder?"

There was a low, distant rumbling.

"That or blasting," said Belle.

"It is thunder," was Cora's opinion. "I hope we can find some shelter."

"Shelter!" exclaimed Bess as she looked anxiously up at the gathering clouds. "How could we ever get the cars under any ordinary shelter?

"That's what I can't get used to about an auto—the size of it. They're like houses to me, as big as all outdoors."

"I know of an old barn out this way, over toward Woodbine," went on Cora. "We would likely find that open, for when I went past there the other day they were getting ready to put the hay in."

"Oh, dear!" exclaimed Belle as the thunder sounded nearer and louder. "I wish we could get back home. Turn around, Bess., dear."

"I can't," declared her sister with a nervous little laugh. "The road is too narrow for me to make a turn in, and I haven't yet learned how to reverse well. We'll have to keep on until I get to a wide place."

"I don't want to do that!" objected Belle. "Let's stop the car, get out, and push it around. Surely we can do that. Don't go any farther."

"Yes, yes!" cried Cora. "Keep on. It's too late to turn back now. There! It's raining! Let me get ahead, and I'll show you the way-a short cut. I know how to get through that lane."

Her car shot ahead, the girl skillfully guiding it, and the twins timidly following, until, with many a twist and turn, Cora piloted them up a little hill to a big red barn, with the wide doors invitingly open.

"Drive right inside," called Cora, slowing down her car. "I guess no one will object, and we haven't any lights to put out, as the warning over the door of the garage says."

The rain was falling in torrents now, and before Cora could get the Whirlwind wholly within the shelter, and while yet the Flyaway was entirely out; the girls received quite a wetting. A moment later they were out of the storm in the barn, had stopped their cars, and shut off the engines.

"Suppose the owner doesn't like it?" suggested Belle.

"Well, we're in, anyway," declared Cora, "and I guess they won't put us out. But we must be careful. Don't let any gasolene or oil drip out. But I guess it won't, as both the cars are new."

No one but themselves seemed to be in the barn, which was odorous with new-mown hay, great mows of it being on either side of the broad floor on which the autos stood.

"There are some men coming," announced Bess, looking out through the big doors into a mist of rain.

"The haymakers," announced Cora. "They were getting in the crop, but the rain didn't let them finish. See how they're running."

"What shall we do when they come in?" inquired Belle, anxiety depicted on her face.

"Why, nothing, I should say," replied Cora. "There is plenty of room for them and us, I'm sure, even if our cars are rather large. We won't eat the men, and I hope they won't eat us."

"Oh, dear!" sighed Belle, but Bess laughed.

The first to reach the barn was a very tall farmer, of the type designated as lean and lanky. He was headed straight for the open doors, his head bent down to avoid the pelting drops, and he did not see the cars and the young ladies until he had nearly collided with Cora. Then he straightened up suddenly, and the look of astonishment on his face made Cora want to laugh, only she felt, under the circumstances, that she did not dare.

"Wa'al, I'll be gum-swizzled!" exclaimed the farmer. "What's this, anyhow? Automobiles? As I live! Wa'al, I swan t' goodness! An' gals a-drivin' of 'em! Ho! ho! Wa'al, that's what I call rich—yes, sir, rich!"

A fringe of curious haymakers gathered behind the one who had entered first.

"We only came in out of the rain," explained Cora, who was looking her prettiest in the confusion. "We hope we're not in the way."

"Oh, you're welcome," the man hastened to say. "As welcome as—wa'al, a heap sight more welcome than this thunderstorm is. We calcalated t' git all th' hay in, but we didn't quite make out. We've got lots of room here, you see. There ain't another barn in all Woodbine that'd take a locomotive like that in it," and he walked around Cora's big car, eying it curiously.

"I knew you had a big barn," said Cora. "I saw it the other day; then, when the storm came, I remembered it, and so we intruded here."

"'Tain't no intrusion, nohow," declared the farmer. "I'm mighty glad of a chance t' git a look at them things close by, when they ain't movin' like a blue streak. My gal is jest daffy about 'em. She thinks it would be handy fer her an' me, but I ruther guess she'd git th' most rides outer it."

"They are very convenient when you want to get somewhere in a hurry," ventured Bess, who thought it time to come to Cora's aid in keeping up the conversation.

"Yes, I expect so; but you see th' trouble on a farm is that you ain't got much of any time t' go anywhere. Now, ef I had a machine like thet—"

There came such a sharp crash of thunder and such a blinding flash of lightning simultaneously that the farmer's voice was silenced, and every one jumped.

"Oh, isn't that awful!" fairly screamed Belle, and instinctively she ran to the side of the tall, lanky man.

"Guess you're used t' bein' near yer pa in a thunderstorm," observed the farmer with a chuckle.

"I thought the barn was struck," said the girl with a shudder. "It would be terrible if it got on fire, with all this hay in it."

"That's what it would; but we're not worryin so much since we got th' new fire apparatus. We've had th' two hose carts for about three weeks now, an' though we've practiced with 'em we ain't never had no real fire. We've got a good water system, with high pressure, an' they can pump more when they need it. All we have t' do is run with those carts t' th' fire, an' attach th' hose t' th' hydrants. But th' funny part of it is that th' carts is so heavy they need hosses t' pull 'em, and we ain't got no reg'lar hosses yet. Have t' pull 'em by hand, I expect, an' it's goin' t' be hard work."

"Do you belong to the department?" asked Cora.

"You're right, I do."

"And is that part of your uniform?" she went on, pointing to some rubber coats and fire hats that hung on the side of the barn.

"Yep, that's what they be. Me an' my two sons. By jimminity crickets! that lightnin' certainly is sharp, though!"

Flash after flash of the glaring light came through the sheets of rain, and the thunder crashed and vibrated overhead, seeming to, shake the very earth.

"Where are your sons?" inquired Belle, wanting too do her share in the talk; but she waited until there came a lull in the storm.

"Over in th' south medder, two miles away," replied the man.

By this time several of the haymakers, seeing that the storm was likely to continue, and knowing that they could no more work that day, had donned heavy coats and departed, going down the road to the village. This left the farmer and one hired man in the barn.

"It certainly is rainin'," remarked the hired man as he looked out through the big doors.

At that instant there came a more terrific crash than any that had preceded it, and the whole place seemed a glare of intense light. Every one was stunned for a moment, and when they recovered their numbed senses, Cora, looking toward the farmhouse, saw a sheet of flame coming from the roof.

"Fire! fire!" she cried. "Your house is afire! It's been struck by lightning!"

"By gum! So it has!" yelled the man. "It's blazing, and my old mother is bedridden in it! Come on, Jake! We'll have t' git her out, anyhow. Now what good is our fire department with no hosses t' haul th' hose carts, an' all my animals away off! Sech luck! Th' men gone, too!"

He was rapidly shouting this as—he ran from the barn.

"Where are the hose carts?" called Cora after him.

"In Si Appleby's barn! A mile away, an' it's a bad road." He pointed to the barn, for it was in sight down the hill.

"Is there a hydrant near your house?"

"Yes. But what good be they without hose?" returned the farmer. He was on the run, halfway to his burning house, the hired man after him.

"We'll bring up the hose carts!" cried Cora.

"We'll pull them with our autos! Come on, Bess—Belle—quick! We must get the hose here! Don't be afraid. Put on the rubber coats and the helmets. The rain can't get through them. The worst of the storm is over now. Oh, I hope they get that poor woman out!

"Hurry! hurry!" she cried as she cranked up her car. "Back your machine out! Reverse it! I'll follow! Let's see what the motor girls can do in an emergency!"

CHAPTER XXII

IDA GILES

Bess really surprised herself by the quickness with which she got her machine out of the barn. In the excitement the words of advice Paul had given her came back with force. In a few minutes the motor girls were rushing down the muddy roads, splashing through big puddles, but they themselves were kept from the drenching downpour by the firemen's heavy coats and helmets. They gave one look back at the burning house. The blaze had enveloped the entire roof.

"Oh, if we can only return in time!" cried Cora as she threw in the full speed forward.

Cora said afterward that they reached the barn in less than four minutes, but Bess declared they never went as fast as that. Mr. Appleby did not know what to make of three excited girls, in two panting automobiles, rushing up to him and demanding the fire apparatus, but—he managed to understand what had happened, and why they wanted it.

"Tie the hose carts to the back of the autos with ropes!" cried Cora. "We can pull them up the hill. Are there any men around to help with the hose? If there are we'll take them to the fire in our cars."

"No, I guess not; but I'll send my boy for some help right away. There'll be lots of men in their houses 'count of the rain. I'll go with you."

Fortunately there was no need to hunt for ropes, as there were two long ones on the hose carts, and Mr. Appleby, working with speed, aided by the girls, soon had the apparatus attached.

The run back took longer, but it—was made in good time, and Cora and Bess, at the wheels of their respective cars, guided them and the hose carts into the yard near the burning house.

The blaze was fiercer now, but it had not eaten down as far as it would have done had it not been for the heavy rain.

The farmer and his hired man had carried the bedridden woman out, placing her on a mattress in the carriage house.

"Attach the hose to the hydrants!" cried Mr. Appleby. "I'll turn on th' water."

"Who'll handle the nozzles?" asked the farmer.

"It'll take two men to each one, there's so much force to th' water."

"You an' I can handle one!" yelled Mr. Apple by, "an' your hired man."

"He can't manage th' other alone."

"Then we'll help!" called Cora. "Come on, girls!"

The lines were unreeled, attached to the hydrants, and were soon spurting water. Cora and Bess, for Belle declared herself too nervous to help, aided the hired man in holding one nozzle of the leaping, writhing hose, that seemed like some great snake as it squirmed under the pressure of the water. The farmer and Mr. Appleby managed the other.

The fire burned slowly, and the little force was really setting it under control when some men, summoned by young Appleby, arrived and relieved the girls. More lines of hose were run from the hydrants, each one of which could supply water to two, and the blaze was soon out, though the house had been considerably damaged.

"Well, if it hadn't been fer them young ladies and their machines, maybe you wouldn't have had any house, Frank," said Mr. Appleby to the farmer.

"That's right; and land knows I can't begin t' thank 'em. If ever they want a friend, all they've got to do is t' call on Frank Ettner——that's me."

He thrust out his rough hand, and Cora clasped—or tried to—the big palm in her own little one.

"I—I don't know how to thank you!" he exclaimed fervently.

"We couldn't help doing it," said Cora, blushing, and then Mr. Ettner insisted on shaking her hand again, and also with Belle and Bess.

"Well, we certainly had an adventure!" exclaimed Cora as the motor girls were riding home after the shower had stopped. "Whatever will the boys say?"

"The boys will be very proud of you, Cora," declared Belle.

It was a few days after this when Cora was out alone in her car, trying to understand, among many other things, why Ida had not called for her ring.

"And why doesn't Jack let me take it to her?" she asked herself again. "I declare I can't understand Jack," and she shook her head.

Along the turnpike she guided her car, going on slow speed to more fully enjoy the odor of the wild honeysuckle which in tangled masses lined the roadside, mingling with the wild rose perfume that was wafted on the gentle breezes.

She came to a narrow place, where there was room but for one vehicle to pass at a time, and seeing a bunch of wild fern, Cora got out of the car to gather some. As she did so she heard a girl's voice pleading in alarmed tones:

"Let me pass! You must let me pass!"

"Not until I get some money out of you—or somebody!" exclaimed the rough voice of a man.

"I tell you I haven't any money!"

"Well, you know who has. Come on, I want it."

There was a sound of breaking sticks, as if the man had taken a step nearer the girl. She retreated, and this brought her into view of Cora.

It was Ida Giles!

Cora leaned forward to catch a glimpse of the man. She was startled to see that he was that good-for-nothing Lem Gildy.

"Come on," growled Lem, "fork over some cash."

"I haven't any. Oh, please, Lem, let me pass!"

He took another step toward her with outstretched hands, and Ids shrank back. She screamed, but Lem only sneered.

"No one'll hear you," he said. "Come on, I must have money, or I'll tell some things I know."

Cora was hidden from the two by a screen of bushes, and on the dirt of the road, with her car running at low speed, they had not heard her.

Lem laid his hand on Ida's wrist.

"Let me alone!" she screamed. "Help! help!"

Cora saw a stout stick lying on the ground. With hardly a thought of what she was doing she caught it up and stepped forward.

"There's nobody here to help you," said Lem with a brutal chuckle.

"Yes, there is!" cried Cora in ringing tones. "Let go of her arm, Lem Gildy, or I'll strike you with this!" and the girl raised the stick over the rascal's head.

He hesitated a moment, still gripping Ida, who was on the verge of collapse. She looked at Cora with wonder and fear.

"Let go!" demanded Cora, taking a step nearer.

"Not for you!" answered Lem defiantly.

Cora brought the stick down with stinging force on his wrist. With a howl of pain he let go and advanced toward Cora, but she struck him aver the head with her weapon, and Ida, who had recovered her courage, catching up a heavy stone, made it a more even battle. With a muttered snarl Lem slunk away and disappeared in the underbrush. Cora felt herself trembling violently, but she kept control of herself.

"Oh, Cora!" sobbed Ida. "I believe I would have died if you had not come along. I was never afraid of Lem Gildy, and when I saw him following me along the road I never dreamed that he would molest me."

"What did he want?" asked Cora.

"Oh, it's all over that dreadful money! Mr. Foster's, you know."

Indeed, Cora was beginning to suspect that.

Sobbing like a child, Ida leaned on the arm that Cora held out to her, though as a matter of fact Cora was in need of assistance herself.

"Well, never mind," she said to Ida. "Just get in my car and we'll go right to your home. He was a perfectly horrid man, and should be punished. See what he did to Jack, starting off his car and injuring him. Now he tries to rob you."

"Not exactly rob, Cora. He says some one—"

"Now don't go into details until you feel better. Come, get in the car with me," and Cora led Ida back to where the auto waited.

"Oh; Cora! I—I can't get in your car with you—I—I can't accept any kindness from you—after—after what I've done. And to think that you should come to save me from him! I—I feel like a—a thief!"

"But you're not!" declared Cora stoutly.

139

"No, not exactly, but almost as bad. Oh, Cora, I—I wish I could tell you, but I—I daren't!" and again Ida sobbed hysterically.

"Well, Ida, dear, you don't have to tell me now—maybe not at any time," spoke Cora soothingly as she placed her arm about the girl's waist. "Come along for a ride in the Whirlwind. That will settle your nerves."

"Where are you going?" asked Ida as she noticed they were not heading for Chelton.

"We'll go to New City, Ida," went on Cora with sudden resolve. "I want to ask you a question."

"Yes," spoke Ida nervously.

"Did you lose anything at my party?" and Cora's thoughts were on the diamond ring in the safe.

"No," replied Ida firmly.

"Didn't you, really?" insisted Cora, surprised that Ida would not admit ownership of the ring.

"I—I didn't lose anything, Cora," and Cora wondered at the stress Ida placed on the word "lose."

"Well, I have a secret to tell you. Jack did not want me to speak of it, but I'm going to, for I'm just consumed with curiosity. Paul Hastings found a beautiful diamond ring in his pocket after the fête, and your initials were engraved in the gold."

Cora turned so as to look into Ida's face, and she could plainly see that a change came over her countenance.

"Paul Hastings found it?" murmured Ida. "The ring with my initials in?"

"Yes. Didn't you really lose it?"

For a moment Ida did not speak. She was biting her lips, and her fingers were nervously playing with the fringe on the lap robe.

"Cora," she exclaimed impulsively, "I have been mean—hateful to you—but—you have not deserved it. Sid Wilcox told me he had you out riding, and he said you spoke of a lot of things about me—"

"What!" cried Cora. "He dared to say that?"

"Yes; and people saw you out with him."

"So they might have; but the truth was he jumped into my car and ran away with it without my permission. That's how I came to be in the motor with him."

"He never told me that!" exclaimed Ida. "Well, that's just like him. Now I will tell you. It was he who forced that ring on me—and I would not take it at first. But he made me. Then I determined to get rid of it. I did not lose it, but I slipped it into Walter Pennington's pocket. Oh, Cora! You know I—I do like Walter, and I—I thought if he saw that I wouldn't keep some one else's engagement ring that—somehow—he might send it back where it came from, and—and—"

Her tears interrupted her. Cora did not understand.

"You put it in Walter Penniniton's pocket?" she repeated slowly. "Why, it was found in Paul Hastings' pocket."

"Wasn't Walter dressed up like Marc Anthony?" demanded Ida, ceasing her sobbing and looking up with wonder in her eyes.

"No. He was the clown. Paul was the Roman," and Cora began to see how some things had come about.

"That explains it," murmured Ida. "It was a mistake! And did that that ring actually have my initials in?"

"It is marked 'I.G.,'" said Cora. "We have been expecting you to call for it."

"Where is it now?"

"Home, in our safe."

"Then keep it there!" exclaimed Ida, a new determination in her voice.

"But we cannot keep it," objected Cora. "It is not mine nor Jack's. Why not give it back to Sid?"

"Neither is it his," went on Ida. "He gave it to me, and now I ask you to keep it—in trust."

"I don't see how we can do that very well. The reason I mentioned it to you, against Jack's wish, was that I wanted to get rid of the responsibility of keeping it. Suppose it should be stolen? It is quite valuable."

"Well, I cannot take it," insisted Ida. "Mother would not allow me to have it in the house. Sid said it cost five hundred dollars."

"It is certainly a very valuable ring," admitted Cora. "But, Ida, if I were you I would give it back to Sid."

"Well, perhaps I shall—some day. But oh, Cora, you cannot imagine what I have gone through with in the last month!" and Ida pressed her handkerchief to her swollen eyes.

"I am sorry," said Cora simply. "Can I help you, Ida?"

They had ridden through New City, and were back again in Chelton. Ida had asked to be let out at the post-office, and as Cora—drew up in front of it for her to alight, Ida extended her hand, and the two girls looked into each other's eyes, each trying to read her neighbor's thoughts.

"Coca, you can help me, and I will soon ask you to do so," said Ida almost in a whisper; "but now—I cannot tell you now," and she hurried out of the car.

CHAPTER XXIII

THE MYSTERY SOLVED

Ida Giles had always been unpopular, and the kindness shown her by Cora Kimball, following opt the timely rescue of her from Lem Gildy, came to the unhappy girl like a revelation.

For the first time in her dissatisfied life Ida determined to do what her better nature prompted her to do, even at the risk of getting into trouble. She determined to clear up the mystery that had been hanging so heavily over the heads of Cora and her friends.

"I—I don't care what Sid thinks—or says," murmured Ida, "I'm done with him forever."

She hurried to a select bowling alley, where she was pretty sure she would find Sid. Within the little office in front one might buy confections or ice cream, and at the same time be able to look in on the alleys, where athletic young men were banging away at the pins. Ida sent in word by the clerk, and Sid came out at once when he heard who wished to speak to him. Ida was struck at his appearance. He looked thin and worn, but, more than that, worried.

"Sid," she began bravely, "you must come with me at once. I will aid you all I can, but we must go right over to the Kimballs', explain everything, and set matters right."

"What!" exclaimed the youth in an anxious whisper. "You mean confess?"

"Yes, that's just it."

"But—but—er—I—"

"I've promised to help you,", she said slowly. They were talking outside now, for the clerk had come back and was behind the showcase. "You must come, Sid, and tell everything. I will do my part. Besides, there is really nothing to confess, you know. You really didn't steal the money, but you must tell them—tell Ed, Cora and all—what you did with it—and about the empty wallet."

"Oh, Ida, I never could do that!"

Sid's bravery—his gay, sneering, bold manner—were all gone. He was a craven—weak. "You'll have to tell them," he added. "I'm going—going away."

"That's just like you!" exclaimed Ida. "Leave me to shoulder all the shame. No, Sid Wilcox! I've risked enough for you! I'm done! If you don't go to the Kimballs' this very afternoon and tell everything, I shall go to the police and relate to them all that I know about the missing money, the bonds and the wallet. The detectives will be glad enough to get the reward."

Sid was really afraid now. His face was pale, and his voice shook as he answered:

"I'll—I'll make it all good now. I have the money. Can't you—can't you give it back to Ed, the way the bonds—"

"No!"

"Not to help me out?"

"No!"

"But you promised—"

"I promised too much! Will you tell everything, or—"

There was a moment's silence. Sid was battling with his mean nature. Even yet he was trying to find a way of escape—to discover some plan by which he could avoid the shame of making a humiliating confession.

"Well?" asked Ida, and there was a new ring in her voice.

"I—I suppose I'll have to," spoke Sid in low tones.

"Come, then. I'll go with you."

An hour later Cora, Jack, Ed, Sid Wilcox and Ida Gales were seated in the library of the Kimball home. Sid was uneasy, and Ida's eyes showed that she had been weeping.

"Sid has something to tell you all," began Ida, "and so have I. I guess you know what it's about."

Cora nodded and smiled at Ida. Then she went over and stood beside the unhappy girl.

"I'll make a clean breast of if, fellows," began Sid hesitatingiy. "I—I really didn't mean to make so much trouble over it, but one thing went to another, and when I started there didn't seem to be any stopping place, or any way to get back.

"When Ed stooped over to fix the mud guard on Cora's car, that day of the race and the collision, the wallet dropped from his pocket into the soft dust of the road. I saw it and picked it up, intending first only to play a joke on him. Ida and Mary Downs saw me, and—well, I don't know what they thought, but I only did it for fun."

"Queer fun," murmured Jack indignantly.

"I slipped out the money and bonds," went on Sid, "and then Ed turned toward me, and I didn't know what to do with the empty wallet. There was only one chance, and I took it. I dropped it in the tool-box of Cora's car. I was mean to do it, for I thought it might make a mix-up and add to the joke."

Jack murmured something inaudible, and Cora shot a warning glance at her brother.

"Yes, it was a poor joke," admitted Sid weakly, "but I've learned a lesson. I found out it was going to cost considerable to fix my car, and as I had some other—er—well, expenses to meet, I just used some of Ed's cash. I knew I could pay it back later.

"That is, I thought I could, but my folks shut down can my allowance, and when I missed getting that job which Paul Hastings got I was in a bad way. I didn't know where I was to get the cash to repay Ed, and I didn't dare say anything, for fear you'd have me arrested for stealing:

"Then I got mixed in with Lem Gildy. He saw me with a lot of cash, and he suspected something. The man is sharp, and one day he saw the numbers of one of the bank notes I had. He looked up the numbers which Ed gave the police, and it corresponded. Then he jumped to the conclusion that I had stolen the ten thousand dollars in cash, and the bonds. Nothing I could say about it being a joke could convince him. He began to bleed me for hush money, and I had to give it to him. Then I thought of a plan for getting him out of the way. I put him up to start Jack's car off, thinking he might be arrested for malicious mischief and put in jail, but I never dreamed you would be hurt, Jack. Honest, I didn't."

Jack did not answer.

"Well, that plan didn't work," went on Sid, "and Lem kept getting worse. Then I didn't know what Mary Downs might be up to, going away as she did. I believe she thought I really stole the money."

"She did," put in Cora. "She told me so; but her going away had nothing to do with it. A relative was taken suddenly ill, and she had to leave. She wrote me something about the robbery—excuse me, I'll not call it a robbery now—but Mary thought it was, and she imagined both Sid and Ida were guilty."

"I can't blame her much," murmured Ida unhappily.

"I have treated you very meanly, Ida," confessed Sid. "I made you keep my secret, and Lem found out—at least, he thought he did—that you were in with me."

"That's why he followed me and demanded money of me," spoke Ida. "I decided then that it must all come out, though I also decided that I would never again have anything to do with you, Sid Wilcox."

"Not even after—" began the youth:

"No. Your—your ring is—here," and she, pointed to the safe.

Sid started.

"I wondered why you didn't wear it," he said: "Yes," he went on, "I have been mean to Ida, though I—I did ask her to take the ring—to—to make up for it."

It was clear that he did care for the girl, as much as it was possible for a person of his selfish nature to care for any one.

"I—I spent some of the money for the ring for Ida," he went on.

"Yes, and for that reason, as much as for any other—because I knew you were only a shade removed from a thief—I threw it away!" burst out Ida.

"When?" asked Sid, much astonished.

"The same night when, masked as a nun, I slipped back the bonds into Ed's pocket—as you asked me to."

"So that's how they got there!" exclaimed Ed.

"Then, when Ida came and told me a little while ago about Lem," went on Sid after a pause, "I knew the game was up. He was getting desperate, and he's liable to send word to the police at any moment, accusing me, and I don't want to be arrested."

He seemed very anxious.

"Now here is your ten thousand dollars back," he said to Ed, handing him a roll of bills. "I managed to get from my folks the amount I had used, including the sum for the—the diamond ring, and what I had to give Lem."

"What's become of him?" asked Jack.

"I guess he's skipped out," answered Sid. "After holding up Ida it won't be safe for him to linger too close to these parts."

"I should say not," commented Cora.

"Now, will you take this money, and—and call it square?" asked Sid nervously.

"Hardly square," murmured Jack. "Look at the suspicions about my sister—"

"Hush, Jack," pleaded Cora, looking at Ida, who was weeping.

"I think the best way will be to call the incident a closed one," decided Ed. "I'll take the money, and—"

"What will you tell the police?" asked Jack.

"I'll tell them the money came back to me in a mysterious way."

"They may want to claim the reward."

"They can't. There is only one person who will get the reward, and she is—"

He paused and walked over until he stood in front of Ida, who sat with bowed head.

"Miss Giles, it is due to you, more than to any, one, that this mystery is solved," he said: "Will you please accept the reward?" and he took some bills off the roll Sid had handed him.

"I couldn't oh, I couldn't!" she sobbed.

Ed looked embarrassed. Every one was under a strain. Jack went to the safe and took out the diamond ring.

"I guess that comes back to you," he said to Sid, "as long as you've made up to Ed the whole sum."

Sid took it hesitatingly. Then with a quick motion he stepped up to Ed.

"Here," he exclaimed, "this belongs to you."

"What for?"

"Interest on your money. It's more than the ring cost, maybe, considering the loss on the bank stock, but I'll make it up later."

"No," said Ed after a moment's thought "We'll call it settled."

He held the ring in his hand and went over to the weeping girl.

"Will you—will you accept this for what you have done for me—for all of us?" he asked gently.

Ida looked up through—her tears. Then she shook her head.

"Let me give it to her," whispered Cora, and Ed handed over the sparkling gem.

"Take it from me, Ida," whispered Jack's sister. "Let it be a pledge of—of whatever you like."

"A pledge from an up-to-date motor girl!" cried Jack gaily, and his words ended the strain that was on them all.

Sid slipped out, and Ida was led away by Cora. Then such talking as there was between Ed and Jack!

"Well, did you ever hear such a yarn?" asked Jack. "Did you suspect him, Ed?"

"Yes, but I thought his motive was a different one. I had an idea the strain would soon tell on him—or Ida. I'm glad it's over."

"So am I!" exclaimed Cora, coming into the room, having parted from Ida. "Oh, I feel years younger!"

"Look out!" warned Ed. "You'll soon be a mere infant again if you keep on."

"I don't care!" she cried. "Come on out and take a long run in the Whirlwind. I want to get some of the cobwebs swept off my brain with a glorious breeze. Come, Jack—Ed."

They went with her, each one happier than they had been in many days.

"Oh! There are Belle and Bess!" cried Cora. "I must tell them."

"Well," remarked Ed, when Cora and Belle had about talked themselves out, "I suppose you motor girls call that quite a series of adventures?"

"Indeed we do," answered Cora. "I don't know that I care to have any more just like them."

But, though no adventures just like those narrated here occurred to the motor girls, the possession of their new cars led them into a strange complication not long afterward, and the details of it will be set down in the next book of this series, to be entitled: "The Motor Girls on a Tour; or, Keeping a Strange Promise."

"Let's have a race!" cried Jack, who was handling the new car of the twins. "Come on, Cora, I challenge you."

"Not now, Jack, dear," replied his sister. "I just want to rest— and think," and she slowed her car down and ran along a quiet country road, with Bess and Jack trailing in the rear.

The end

Made in the USA